PENGUIN BOOKS

BEYOND BELONGING

Judy Liu's purpose is to help people live courageously as their weird and wonderful selves. For a time, she lived out of a suitcase while being the Head of Learning & Development for a UK listed company—bouncing between hotels, bunkbeds, airport lounges, and couches. Now, running her own leadership consultancy, The Outlier Mind, she helps leaders bravely connect with their inner knowing. A self-leadership coach with a background in organizational psychology, she is deeply curious about what happens when people shed themselves of expectations and confront uncomfortable truths—but most importantly, a believer that we were born knowing who we are, but we spend our lives forgetting.

Born in Taiwan, brought up in Thailand and Australia, and spending most of her career in Singapore, the belonging she struggled with as a kid became her greatest strength. When her role was made redundant in June 2024 after ten years of service, her most memorable farewell message from a senior leader was, 'I'm really going to miss your outspokenness,' for she always stood for what people felt but didn't dare say.

As you step into the realm of *Beyond Belonging*, she invites you to reimagine your life from the inside out.

ADVANCE PRAISE FOR *BEYOND BELONGING*

Beyond Belonging is a heartfelt journey that resonates deeply with me. Judy's words capture the complexities of identity, home, and belonging with such honesty and grace. Through her storytelling. I felt seen, as if she had given voice to experiences many of us have carried quietly within. A truly inspiring read that touches both the mind and the heart.'

—Ratna Juita
Founder, The Mindgem

Beyond Belonging

Judy Liu

PENGUIN BOOKS
An imprint of Penguin Random House

PENGUIN BOOKS

Penguin Books is an imprint of the Penguin Random House group of companies whose addresses can be found at global.penguinrandomhouse.com

Published by Penguin Random House SEA Pte Ltd
40 Penjuru Lane, #03-12, Block 2
Singapore 609216

Penguin Random House SEA

First published in Penguin Books by Penguin Random House SEA 2025

10 9 8 7 6 5 4 3 2 1

ISBN 9789815323092

Typeset in Garamond by MAP Systems, Bangalore, India

www.penguin.sg

To all those curious about living life as our weird and wonderful selves.

To Venerable Master Hsuan Hua, Derren Brown, and the universe. A monk, mentalist and magical force. None of them know me (I suppose the universe does) however, all have inspired me to be courageous in doing things differently.

Contents

How to Use This Book

This book is your playground, and you can roam through it in several ways. I call these options Reading, Reflecting and Beyonding. While the first two are self-explanatory, 'Beyonding' refers to the playful endeavour of connecting with your truth through artistic, creative means.

If you like context, start with Reading then work your way through Reflecting and Beyonding. Or if you are curious and courageous, start with Beyonding, then decide later if you want to go through Reading and Reflecting.

Each component builds on the other, but where you start and end is entirely up to you. The only thing I would suggest is that you someway, somehow, make your way to Beyonding. Some of the activities may feel weird and uncomfortable, but the whole point of Beyonding is to go to places you wouldn't normally go.

Take a breath, enjoy the adventure, and play in the way that calls out to you.

1. **Reading:** Stories and studies exploring each chapter's concept
2. **Reflecting:** Summary of concept, questions to ponder & self-coaching exercises
3. **Beyonding:** Whimsical activities that ignite a sense of wildness and wonder, while bringing you home to your truth

Introduction

Do you want to find that place you 'belong' to?

The place you can always call home, where you will be accepted exactly as you are; the place that will inspire your growth, boost your creativity, and expand your worldview. The good news is that many places claim to offer it: organizations promoting their close-knit family cultures, communities that open their arms to you, and hold you like a warm blanket. Or that special person, whom you snuggle with and feel like, *Ahh . . . everything is perfect when I'm with you.*

There's no denying—belonging feels great! And when things feel great, we do whatever we can to prolong it. We hold onto it, reliving it in our minds the love, the words said, and the feeling of being valued, polishing the scene over and over until it shines brighter than reality ever allowed.

But there's also some bad news: the side of belonging we shy away from.

We spend our lives attaching our identity to people, organizations, and communities, believing that it solidifies our existence into the world. We cling to it like our most prized possession, defending it, even when it hurts us. We lie to ourselves when it steers us off-course, and we allow it to shape and reshape us so many times till we forget who we are.

Then one day, we get stuck.

We ask ourselves questions like, 'Who am I?' and 'What am I doing this for?' A sense of meaninglessness sinks in as we start to wonder whether life is but a pointless exercise where, in the end, we die. Some refer to this feeling as 'existential crisis', to which there are two common responses: first, ignore it and let that sense of loss linger in the background; the second, venture into an eat-pray-love journey of 'finding' yourself.

However, we rarely link that great feeling of belonging to this sense of loss, because they cannot share a strain, right?

Belonging = good, existential crisis = bad.

So there can't possibly be a connection between these two vastly separate concepts, we tend to think.

What if I told you that there is a connection?

What if I told you there is a dark side to belonging that most of us choose not to acknowledge? It's like selectively choosing to only see half the pie, then attributing the other half to something completely different when it reveals itself.

In his book *No Mud, No Lotus* Vietnamese monk and peace activist Thich Nhat Hanh says, 'There can be no lotus flower without the mud.'[1] Equally, there is a price we pay for belonging, and we need to awaken to what that is.

Belonging is like a campfire: the warmth draws us in, we feel safe in its light and the shared glow connects us. But if we get too close, we'll get burned, and if you stay too long, you forget how to find your own light. Both sides of the fire teach us, and recognition of both sides allows us to enjoy it without losing ourselves in it.

In a study conducted on 1600 children, it was found that 98 per cent of children between the ages of four to five showed the potential for creative genius. When these children reached the age of ten, that number dropped to 30 per cent; at fifteen, it fell further down to 12 per cent. As adults, that number plummets to 2 per cent.[2]

The author of the study, George Land, concluded that we were born creative, yet we subsequently learn non-creative behaviour through the way we are socialized. As we age, our imagination diminishes, our creativity depletes, and we grow 'dependent on right answers, that are repeatable, that are predictable,' as Land puts it.

However, while it may feel like we have lost a superpower, the bright side is, we still have a chance to gain it back. That five-year-old version of us, bursting with creativity, left us a trail to reverse our conditioning. If we can learn to understand the invisible forces that boxed us in, we can navigate them to set ourselves free.

I grew up in several places—Taiwan, Thailand, Australia, and Singapore, and have always been intrigued by how differently people perceive the world. As a high school student in Sydney, I used to tutor an eight-year-old boy for extra pocket money. At the end of one of our sessions, after we had packed up and gone downstairs to meet his mom, he suddenly turned around and said, 'Judy, can I ask you a question?'

His mom smiled, encouraging him to continue. He then proceeded to say, 'You know, *your* type of people . . .' (The little rascal was referring to Asians, I assumed.) Immediately, his mom's expression shifted to one of awkward discomfort.

But I responded calmy. 'Yes, Nick?'

'You know, how your eyes are like this,' he said, using his fingers to show me how my eyes were narrower and longer than his.

His mom, now visibly horrified, started nudging him to stop. But I smiled at her, assuring her that I was not offended; in fact, I was genuinely curious about what he was going to ask next.

'Yes?'

I saw his eyes light up knowing that he could finally ask something he had clearly been thinking about for some time. Then, with pure innocence and childlike wonder, he dropped the question: 'Do you see the world like we see it?'

It stopped me in my tracks. My mind drew a complete blank. I was stumped. 'I don't know,' I replied honestly. 'Maybe I do. Actually, I've never thought about it.'

Excited by my response, he burst out with one more. 'Maybe, you see your life like a movie—like in the cinemas, where there is a widescreen!'

I was blown away.

I had really never thought about it, and I could totally see how different eye shapes could lead to different ways of seeing the world. For example, I remember learning in primary school that animals, whose eyes are further apart, have greater peripheral vision, and those with large forward-facing eyes take in light better, helping them focus on prey.

Yet, while we explore it openly when talking about animals, we have become so sensitive to discussing anything about human differences, possibly in fear of being seen as discriminatory. So, we often end up ignoring the topic altogether. We do the same with politics, religion, and culture—just to name a few.

The open floor of conversation is littered with eggshells, and it's easier to retreat to surface-level interactions—any extension of curiosity beyond that poses a great risk of being shut down, ridiculed, or judged. Our efforts to respect another person's model of the world has translated to avoidance and silence, replacing dialogue. This is the fastest way to perpetuate segregation.

But thanks to little Nick' imagination, my mind was abruptly stretched to a place I wouldn't have otherwise gone to. I drove home that day with a curiosity about all the other things that are right in front of us, but never questioned.

As we learn the ways of the world, we leave behind the maps of our hearts, and turn down the volume on that little voice we once followed instinctively as kids. We send away our imaginary friends, cut off the wildness of our edges, and traded in our creative wonder for professionalism, maturity, and responsibility. We introduce ourselves by our job titles, speak definitively about who we are and what we do.

Yet, have we really grown up? Are we *really* older and wiser? Or have we just suppressed the parts of ourselves which didn't fit the mould in exchange for acceptance and belonging?

We are taught to reduce the vibrancy of who we are, so we fit into neat little boxes. We create illusory versions of ourselves, marked by the labels given to us by cultures, communities, and companies. We learn about what people expect from us, and are rewarded when we follow suit. Falling in line is accepted as a contribution to the collective, while being an outlier a mark of selfishness. Long standing expectations are rarely challenged, and when we feel conflict within, we push it into the darkness and carry on. We slip into a state of unconscious living, where our bodies are alive but our minds are asleep in blind obedience.

As kids, we are given a definition of success: a job with a high paying salary, for instance. At school, we are channelled through rigid pathways, where academia is held on a pedestal and vocational studies are for those who fell short. As adults, at work, we carry out instructions from leaders, even if they feel unethical or against our values. We might make some noise, but often, we quieten down, as the system is too hard to change. At the same time we juggle expectations from our community, culture, and family. The culmination of it all leads to a life that never feels quite right, and yet, we keep going.

It's akin to Milgram's study of obedience, where people continued to administer increasingly stronger electric shocks to another person, even as they screamed and begged for them to stop.[3] 'Ignore the signs, follow the process.' Everyone else is doing it, so it should be right . . . right?

The combination of authority and trust is so powerful, it can lead us to engage in activities that are incongruent with our moral compass. Yet, this is not just a study. We live and breathe these unseen forces every day, even denying their existence. We say that we were 'just following orders,' rationalizing the dissonance by convincing ourselves that it was the 'right' thing to do, and disuniting our identities from our actions. Instead of turning up our awareness to what's going on, we turn down our intuition and keep going. We rack up a lifetime of rules and norms, letting them dictate our lives as we run on autopilot.

Then, there are the shadows.

Like physical shadows that are created when the light is covered, we build up psychological shadows: the unconscious aspects of our being we hide from the outside world. For example, a family where harmony and respect for elders is paramount, strong emotions and any challenges to traition are discouraged. To uphold the collective want for harmony, feelings of anger, confusion, and frustration are left in the darkness with no avenue for redress. This can evolve into a belief that emotions threaten belonging, inadvertently shunning all feelings. Likewise, in an environment where excellence is the expectation, we quickly learn that there is no place for expression of weakness.

Dwelling in self-doubt and fears of being inadequate, we are eaten alive from the inside—all the while projecting a picture-perfect façade. We're conditioned to focus on what's tangible; so, when our shadow selves surface as repeated patterns of destructive behaviour, we attribute it to external circumstances, rather than delveing inwards to understand how they came to be. We prioritize *going* through life over *growing* through life, fixating on what is outside of us rather than the true common denominator: ourselves.

That is the system we belong to, and it's addictive.

Linking every part of our being to people and places can feel nurturing and comforting, with the feeling of togetherness shielding us in challenging times. However, we must take off our rose-tinted glasses to confront the whole truth. This includes seeing the invisible forces that stifle our ability to make sound decisions, the attachment we develop to the approval of others, and the lengths we are willing to go to betray ourselves so we can preserve our belonging.

We like to believe that we lead the charge in our lives, but like the man riding an elephant, it is the four-legged creature—our unconscious mind—that is really in control, a hidden realm where experiences, expectations, and influences quietly guide our every move. Our unconscious mind is a vast storage unit, weaving together patterns based on everything it has gathered from our lives: what people have said to us, what we have seen others do, what happens to those who disobey. It silently steers us in ways we may not fully recognize or understand.

However, if we become cognizant of how it influences our lives, we can loosen its hold on us, and trace the trail back to a version truer to ourselves. When we can awaken to the invisible workings of our world, we can move fluidly within the bounds of belonging and beyond.

Wake up, little bird. It's time to fly.

Chapter 1

CONFORMITY

We all like to think of ourselves as independent thinkers, right?

'I don't follow the crowd', we reaffirm, mentally patting ourselves on the back. 'I think for myself, no one tells me what to do!'

News flash!

We are more susceptible to influence and conformity than we'd like to admit.

Follower Mentality

In a social experiment, an unknowing participant enters an eye clinic and is seated in the waiting room along with other patients.[4] Unaware that those around her are actors, she takes her seat, picks up a magazine, and settles in. The sound of a beep goes off, and for some strange reason, everyone stands up and sits back down. No words are spoken; no explanation given.

The beep goes off once more. Again, the rest of the patients stand up and sit back down. While the test subject watches others with a face of uncomfortable curiosity and confusion, she has clearly noticed the pattern: beep = stand up.

What would you do if you were in her shoes?

Most of us would probably laugh and say, 'That's wild! I would never fall for that.' Yet, in just three beeps, and with no understanding of why she is standing up, the test subject begins to perfectly conform to the behaviour of the group. Unknowingly, she has succumbed to the unspoken pressure of social conformity.

To stretch this even further, the actors are called into the doctor's office one by one, eventually leaving her alone in the waiting room.

But what happens next, when there is no one around her to reinforce the unspoken rule?

The beep goes off . . . and . . . she stands up again!

She continues to conform to the rules of the group, even after all of them have left, continuing to stand up and sit down with each beep, as other unknowing participants arrive. Miraculously, one by one, they follow suit with this unexplained behaviour—of which she has, subsequently, become the leader for.

Jonah Berger, a professor at the University of Pennsylvania, explains this internalized form of herd behaviour as 'social learning'. Just as children learn from the behaviour of others, our brains, as adults, also reward us for conforming. We are wired to being socialized; hence, we have a natural inclination to follow the crowd, even if we're not consciously aware of it.

Think of the last time you stepped into a crowded elevator.

While there are no signs or written rules about how and where you should stand, everyone stands facing the same direction: the door. Now, imagine you step into that elevator again, but this time, you consciously make the decision to face the back of the elevator while everyone else continues to face the door.

As you are the only one doing this, without anyone saying a word, you can feel the weight of judgement for going against the grain. While you hold this mental picture, notice how you feel.

Now, in that picture, turn yourself around. This time, imagine you are facing the door, just like everyone else. Notice how your body relaxes, and the relief and assurance you feel upon doing the 'right' thing.

These are the benefits of being socialized: the feeling of safety and comfort in knowing that we fit in with what everyone else is doing.

Since we are rewarded for conformity, we naturally gravitate towards it. We do it so much without even realizing, often trapping ourselves in habit loops, reinforcing them continually through unconscious mirroring of other people's behaviour. We then continually pass down these behaviours with no apparent rhyme or reason. 'It is how it is,' we tell ourselves. Even for those who are more aware of what's happening, the discomfort of not conforming can be so intense that over time, it wears down our resistance and we fall in line—albeit reluctantly.

Learned Helplessness

This links to another psychological phenomenon called 'learned helplessness'. This is when we give up trying to go against the grain because we believe nothing we do will change the outcome.

In a study conducted by psychologist Martin Seligman, dogs were exposed to electric shocks. Some dogs could stop the shocks by pressing a button with their nose; others continued to receive them, irrespective of what they did. For the dogs in the second group, their initial struggles to escape soon turned into passive behaviour where they stopped trying, even when escape became possible.[5]

Over time, the dogs learned that their behaviour and outcomes are independent—that nothing they do would alter the circumstances. Hence, they resorted to doing nothing at all.

Similar research has been conducted on cats, rats, fish, monkeys, and humans, and it is generally accepted that whenever we sense uncontrollability, our readiness to respond to trauma deteriorates. We take what we're given, we let life happen to us, and we allow it to continue—even when later options emerge for us to choose differently.

When we understand this concept of learned helplessness alongside conformity, we realize that even when we want to do things differently, or feel the calling of something beyond the norm, the pressure to conform to the group can be so high that we eventually give in, feeling powerless to our circumstance.

We see this at workplaces, where people give up on sharing their opinions, choosing to instead stay silent or nod even when they disagree. We also see this in relationships, where the parties have given up on communicating with each other, choosing to accept a life of feeling unseen and misunderstood. Somehow, we convince ourselves that this is but a normal part of life, casting ourselves as helpless incapable people in a predetermined reality.

Pressure and Encouragement

Social psychologist Solomon Asche conducted a famous study demonstrating how conformity functions.[6]

In his experiment, participants were shown a set of lines and asked to identify which one matched the length of another. While it appeared to be a test for the group, there was only one real participant. Unknown to them, the remaining participants were confederates, placed in the group to deliberately give wrong answers. The test was easy—the differentiation between the lines were clear. However, even though the correct answer was obvious, 75 per cent of participants ended up conforming to the group's obviously incorrect answer at least once. Over a third of participants answered incorrectly every time the group did. This is comparable to the less than 1 per cent error rate from the control participants who answered with no group present.

The pressure to fit in—even when it's blatantly incorrect—can be incredibly strong. So, when the majority around us appear to have drunk the Kool-Aid, we might first object to it. However, it's highly likely that, over time, we begin to unconsciously align our mindset with theirs. We may resign ourselves to the justification that 'This is just the way things are,' and stop looking for solutions—all the while reinforcing learned helplessness. If we do this enough, we grow so accustomed to behaving *unlike* ourselves, that we start believing that version as who we really are.

We assume the group's beliefs and call it belonging, as fooling ourselves into thinking we are in the right place is easier than being reminded that the life we had envisioned for ourselves as kids was greater than our reality. Call it childish, foolish—whatever you like, but there are parts of us we have sacrificed for the sake of conformity, and we've grown so used to it that we are now that helpless dog, sitting in stillness, even when there is a chance to escape.

This is an important realization because we are all constantly subject to invisible forces that shift and change the way we behave—sometimes knowingly, sometimes completely otherwise. Conformity is our nature; it's baked into our biology. We're social animals designed to seek out belonging, to be taken in as a member of a tribe. While we may not conform in every way, if we deny its existence in our lives, we'll never give ourselves the choice to move beyond it. To take the reigns of our life, we must first admit that the elephant we are riding is actually the one running the show.

They say when you buy a red car, you suddenly start noticing all the red cars on the road. Using the same principle, the path to freedom begins with acknowledgement. If we can accept that we are natural conformists, surrounded by constant forces around us at work, we can tune our sensitivity to become more aware of what's happening.

Too many of us are trapped in the confines of what we believe is the *only way*. Be it for responsibility, duty, or living up to expectations, each time we close off possibilities, we narrow our world. We lose our ability to imagine a life beyond the rules we were told to live by, shutting off all other options to the point where we trap ourselves in: tolerating an abusive marriage for the sake of cultural expectations; enduring a career you have no interest or talent in for the sake of face; placing immense strain on your emotional well-being for the sake of filial piety. While social learning is a critical part of our development, social *unlearning* is the permission we give ourselves to reclaim our lives.

Conformity and belonging come hand in hand. We conform to feel a sense of belonging. When we belong, we conform even more. It's the seductive whisper in your ear telling you, 'Go ahead; just blend in. It'll be easier that way.' It feels safe and comfortable, like your favourite sweater that's just a little too worn in, yet feels *so* familiar. It's the voice that tells you, 'Everyone is doing it, so you must too.' The familiar Asian parent threat of 'What would people think of you if you . . .' is the social proof that keeps us in line with everyone else.

We follow career paths because they're 'practical' or expected, not because they light us up from the inside. We scroll through social media, liking and commenting, because . . . well, everyone else is doing it, right? It's not even like we're *trying* to conform; it just happens. One behavioural trend leads to another, then another—till we're walking on autopilot to places far from where we wanted to go.

Mentalist Derren Brown demonstrated this in a scary Netflix show *The Push,* where he tested whether social pressure could manipulate a normal human being into committing a crime as heinous as murder.

In a room full of seventy other actors, the unknowing participant, Chris, navigates through a series of scenarios that pressure him to obey an authority. Each scenario feeds into the other, as he is nudged to take on increasingly immoral acts, building up to the last act of pushing an old millionaire off a building.

It utilizes the influencing technique of social compliance, illustrating the delicate and terrifying power of small decisions. The subtle encouragement of a small action, a few seemingly innocent requests that formed the stepping stones to riskier asks: picking something up, switching out labels, keeping quiet when mistakes were made. Each moment of discomfort is met with gentle encouragement from a figure of authority, and the logical continuation of the scenarios meant nothing felt too overt or sudden. Each act of obedience builds momentum, making Chris more invested in the course of action. Then, before he realizes it, the requests have escalated, and he is faced with a decision that, in any other context, would never be considered.

Without spoiling it for you, let's just say that we are far more malleable than we think, and when we become part of a system, we are so thoroughly entwined in it that it blurs our moral compass. Even if we feel like we are still in control of our own choices, we may already be on the brink of doing something unimaginable. Perhaps, the scariest truth is that the principles behind *The Push* aren't limited to the extremes of television stunts or psychological experiments—they are present in our lives, right in this moment.

In any social dynamic—at work, in relationships, in your community—there is always a sequence of small seemingly insignificant decisions that were building to something larger. Its influence is rarely aggressive or overt: more like the soft tug of a current beneath the surface. From a young age, we were taught to fulfil certain roles, whether we realize it or not. Perhaps, you were always the 'responsible' one in the family—the child who followed the rules, who helped with chores, who got good grades. At first, this role is something you might take on willingly, even proudly. It feels natural. But over time, as your family begins to expect more of you, the pressure quietly increases with each passing year. Each time you agree to help, each time you step in to take care of something, you're building momentum toward becoming the person they depend on.

The shift is subtle: One day, you look around and realize that you're not just helping out of kindness anymore, you're *expected* to. Your sense of autonomy blurs; you feel selfish if you prioritize yourself. What started as a small favour has now become a pattern—a role you play without ever asking yourself if you wanted it. The longer you stay in that role, the harder it becomes to step out of it.

Your family—whether consciously or not—pushes you further down the path, until the very idea of stepping away feels like betrayal. The offhand comment like 'You're the responsible one; you know better,' or 'You're the one who always takes care of things,' can be enough to keep you locked in the pattern. It's not a single, direct request—it's a series of quiet nudges, each one reinforcing your role within the family system.

But now, you have a family of your own, and your partner and children's need for you conflicts with your parents' expectation that you'll always be there. You burn yourself to the ground trying to cater to everyone, falling short in your role as the 'responsible' and capable one you've always been. You judge yourself for not being good enough; you work harder, losing all sense of self in the process.

Now, let's take a side-step into the workplace.

You are in an organization where it felt like you fit naturally. You have great colleagues and the environment feels supportive.

You proudly acknowledge that you belong, even deeming the workplace as your second home.

Then comes the first restructure.

You lose a few colleagues, and the business has no intention to replace them. You are asked to take on a new set of tasks on top of your regular responsibilities. It seems harmless, maybe even a chance for you to step up and shine.

Over time, the requests increase—each one a little more than the last. You're commended as the person who always goes the extra mile: the loyal, dedicated, and reliable employee. You convince yourself it's good exposure, showing you're taking initiative and that you're invested in the company's success. But the nudges bring on more and more work—until one day, you realize you're doing the work of three people. But now there's no thank-yous and appreciation; it's become an expectation. To go back to a reasonable workload is now perceived as a drop in performance: You could do it before, so why not now?

What has also become an expectation is our acceptance of the company's chosen path as our own, to go along with what is given, even if you have doubts. What once felt like an optional commitment now feels like a requirement. 'Everyone is on board with this change,' becomes a reminder that stepping out of line feels like you're not supporting the group. The people who used to speak up have quietened down too.

You start to think within the narrow confines of the situation. 'This is all I can do,' you tell yourself. Caught in the grip of survival, you give into the environment, allowing it to shape you into believing there is no way out: you reach a place of uncontrollability. You stop questioning whether you want to accept the change. And so, the door to possibilities slowly closes, and your self-belief becomes smaller than your potential.

Until one day, your friend from outside the organization shakes you and asks, 'What happened to you? What happened to all the things you stood for?'

But, by now, changing course feels too great of a feat. You're committed, and somehow, it feels like that decision was made for you. Even when you realize you've drifted far from your original intentions, the desire to not rock the boat starts to overpower your ability to assert your own preferences. You tell yourself you're still in control, but something in you knows you're far from it, but it's too confronting to face. The excuses feel much more comfortable. So, you ignore your friend and keep going because this is your identity now.

Learned helplessness in full force.

The Pattern

Our work is to identify our conformist patterns. Sometimes they are obvious, oftentimes they are not. Run through your typical day, in as much detail as possible. You can write it down if it helps. What forces are at play in your daily life?

If we choose to live in oblivion, it will shrink us down to that 2 per cent creativity that George Land found in adults. On the surface, doing what we're told seems simpler, safer, even easier. But at some point, the question needs to change. The casual 'What are you doing these days?' is not sufficient in measuring anything real. The question that matters becomes your own: What am I *really* doing with my life?

It's quite the paradox, where the smarter we get, the dumber we get. Our knowledge and 'maturity', while undoubtedly important, conditions us to suppress the wisdom that our physical senses and instincts provide. We sharpen our cognitive abilities and are rewarded for being *logical.* Meanwhile, sensing and feeling are often dismissed as *illogical,* pushing us to disengage from the signals our bodies are constantly sending.

At work, our promotion of well-being is often reduced to three external Fs: fruits, flu shots, and fitness, with very few going above and beyond to help people connect to the essence of a life well lived, with the three Ms: meaning, motivation, and mentoring. We sleep less, have less soul enriching conversations, and eat food that doesn't nourish us. We create our own psychosis as we opt for doom scrolling when our bodies are desperately needing rest, to digest, and rejuvenate. We have been led into an endless pursuit of success and, in the process, lost touch with the very vessel through which we experience it.

However, this is not a new phenomenon—rather a gradual path of conformity we have been walking down for years. The more knowledge we accumulate, the more we sever the connection to the intuitive wisdom that once anchored us. We leave behind that five-year-old that played based on how they felt. Our senses—touch, taste, sight, smell, and hearing—were once the primary means by which we experienced and understood the world. They were our guides, helping us navigate everything from basic survival to emotional health. Now, we use our minds to solve problems that our bodies could have already provided answers to. We medicate in order to suppress symptoms without ever addressing its core cause.

We are constantly taught, right from childhood, that to be successful, we must push harder, work longer, and optimize every minute of our day. Our children can be subjected to endless classes while adults get endless meetings—all the while measuring our value in this world through test scores and salaries. We become so adept at intellectualizing every aspect of our lives that we forget how to simply *be*: to be present and grounded in the here and now.

Take a breath. Listen for the furthest thing you can hear. Keep doing this for ten seconds. Now listen for the closest thing you can hear. Do this for another ten seconds. What did you notice?

In any spare moment we have, instead of reconnecting with our being, we squeeze in another post, another email, another errand. Eventually, later in life, we end up feeling like we have lost ourselves. We become fragmented beings, belonging to groups of *other* fragmented beings. However, instead of seeing the need to reevaluate the system, we bask in the comfort of being a part of a group of other people who are *just like us.*

The road beyond belonging is not easy, but I hope you've come to feel the necessity for it. This is not a calling for mass rebellion and havoc, but rather, an invitation from one human being to another—we can be so much more than what this system has taught us.

I am still on that journey myself, and am grateful to walk alongside you as you begin yours.

REFLECTING

Conformity is not always a choice. We're constantly guided by invisible forces unbeknownst to us. Small seemingly insignificant decisions slowly build a path toward conformity. Overtime, these choices accumulate and the influences that had once nudged us become what we decide is us.

We are all conditioned to achieve, be the best, and to stay in our heads and out of our bodies. We sleep less, eat poorly, and ignore the cues our body gives us. All this, because apparently that's the definition of success. Yet, when we get there we wonder why it doesn't feel quite right. The path to waking up and going beyond belonging is a difficult yet important one, and it starts with recognizing that we are all part of a system.

Ponder

- Where in my life have I unconsciously allowed my environment to define my choices?
- When was the last time I truly listened to my body?
- If we took a step back and asked, 'Am I truly in control of my life?', what would the answer be?

Be Your Own Self Coach

Reflect on a current role that you sense misalignment in; perhaps, it is your role in the family, society, organization, community, or a relationship. Ask yourself: How did I come to occupy this role? What were the invisible forces of influence at play that I couldn't see back then? What pressures do I feel to maintain this role? In connecting with my senses, what is my body telling me about this?

If you retrace your steps, what patterns of behaviour or thinking do you notice? When are you most susceptible to influence? In which situations do you feel the most pressure to conform? What signals has your body given you that you have ignored? How can you be more aware if this occurs again in future?

Beyonding

Complete each bird by joining the dots. Use a thin pen to ensure you get it as exact as possible.

Now make **one** a weird and wonderful bird. Ruffle its feathers, give it an outfit, and colour it crazy! Let it be the expression of you that you only let out when you feel completely safe. Now, tear this page out of the book and stick it somewhere visible. Take a photo of it and make it your screensaver on your phone. Let it constantly remind you that amid conformity, there is a weird and wonderful version of you, right here, within you.

Chapter 2

THE PSYCHOLOGY OF BELONGING

We are all born with an innate desire to belong, driven by the subtle yet powerful force of conformity. This moulds our choices, thoughts, and actions. It is the silent architect of our lives which entices us to fit in, to gather, and be a part of the collective.

No matter how fiercely we guard our independence, we all crave the warmth of being seen, accepted, and valued. The security of being part of something greater, where we fit in more comfortably in the world, is the magnetism of belonging that makes life feel complete.

As we sink into that image of completeness, let me poke some holes in it. This is aimed at forcing us to open our eyes a little wider, to see the scene a little clearer.

Here are a few thought-provoking myths around the psychology of belonging.

Chapter 2.1 – Safety in Numbers

From an evolutionary perspective, being part of a group provides shared resources, safety in numbers, and protection from external threats. We feel a sense of comfort and reassurance in knowing that we are not alone. Tracing our lineage back to our ancestors, we find that tribes shared rituals, sang songs that carried in the wind, and etched their stories on stones to mark their solidarity. They fought alongside one another, and each tribe pulsed with the heartbeat of its people; each member playing their part in a choreography of bonding and survival.

Anthropologist Robin Dunbar suggested that early human societies operated within close-knit groups of up to 150 people.[7] This is known as the Dunbar's Number, a theoretical limit to the number of meaningful and stable relationships one can maintain. While it has been argued that this number fluctuates depending on culture and context, it offers insight into the magnetism that draws people together in community cohesion and protection.

Fast forward to our hyper-connected present, the solidarity of belonging has evolved into something quite different. In large, congested cities, we find ourselves surrounded by crowds; yet, if we peel back the busyness, a tenuous feeling of disconnect lurks beneath the surface: neighbours pass each other in silence in lobbies; a smile to a stranger is often returned with an odd look of confusion; and office lifts are strictly non-conversational, unless you happen to be from the same company. You may live in a high rise with 150 units, surrounded by noise from every angle, and yet describe it as living 'alone'.

So, what about this perceived safety in numbers?

On 13 March 1964, Kitty Genovese was returning home in New York from work, when she was viciously attacked in a parking lot. She screamed for help while being repeatedly stabbed. For a moment, she managed to escape and ran towards her apartment; however her assailant caught up to her. She died from the brutality of the second attack.

A detailed article on *The New York Times* reported that as many as thirty-eight people had seen or heard the attack, yet not a single person intervened or called the police. There was outrage and confusion over how so many people could remain passive in the face of such violence. The incident sparked questions about the dynamics of group behaviour and the psychological phenomenon known as the bystander effect.

While later details revealed that it may not have been as bleak as it was portrayed in the news—like, for instance, the police had been contacted yet failed to show up; people presumed her to be drunk; each passerby had expected the other to step in and help; or simply, they had refrained from helping due to personal reasons—the reality is, it's common for people to stand back and watch rather than help in times of crisis. A fight breaks out, and our instinctive action is often to pull out our phones to record the commotion.

Our preference to witness events, rather than help, also extends to online spaces. The modern bystander effect—social media witnessing, in today's context—means that we will witness harmful actions such as online harassment, bullying, or hate speech and choose not to intervene, despite the availability of tools to report or speak out. Whether it is because we are desensitized from the intensity of emotions we frequently see online, a fear of social backlash, or we simply can't be bothered, 'safety in numbers' is much more an illusion than an ironclad concept.

Belonging to a community doesn't guarantee safety, even when surrounded by many. While it may appear that there is a sense of shared responsibility, it creates a false sense of security where we assume others will act when we are in need. In examining the legitimacy of 'safety in numbers', we must also consider the psychological mechanisms at play. The more people present in a situation, the less likely any single individual is to act. We 'belong' to the group, not the outlier. So, if members of the group aren't acting, we do the same. This collective mindset dulls our instincts, convincing us that someone else will intervene, and if we don't, it's fine because other people didn't either.

This begs one question: Does belonging blind us to complacency? Is it a disguise of safety?

Consider this in the context of redundancies—the rolling surges of workforce reductions felt by millions. In fact, we all probably have a lengthy list of people whose lives were impacted—or it may have been our personal experience.

While not comparable to the brutal murder of Kitty Genovese, it carries a similar collective silence of the bystander effect. The more surprising thing is, these are not the strangers you live 'alone' in an apartment with, but rather the colleagues with whom you shared genuine connection—or so you thought.

Take yourself back to a round of layoffs made in your office: The palpable tension in the air, the nervous glances, and deafening silence of unspoken words. Everyone is playing a game of freeze tag. Your departing colleague gathers their possessions—the weight of hurt and uncertainty heavy on their shoulders. They shuffle past familiar desks adorned with motivational posters about team spirit and support. Their colleague, who they had coffee with yesterday, pretends to be busy in the corner, avoiding eye contact like it's a competitive sport.

In this moment of pain and loneliness, instead of receiving a chorus of support, the departing colleague encounters a wall of silence. Perhaps, there is survivor's guilt for the colleague lurking in the corner; yet the thought of stepping forward to offer genuine warmth in this time of need feels too daunting. They rationalize their silence, telling themselves, 'Maybe, they need space. I don't know what to say, and it's not my place to intervene.'

The avoidance is laced with a touch of irony. In an age where we're conditioned to be hyper-connected, where transparency and authenticity is all the craze, the workplace can become a peculiar arena for emotional disconnection. The fervent celebrations at parties, along with posts of solidarity on social media, quickly switches to passive silence at times when it matters the most.

Perhaps, this also speaks to the fragility of belonging. However, before we think all hope is lost, we might, if we're lucky, catch a glimpse of one brave soul—an outlier amid the frozen crowd. They come forward, embrace the parting colleague with a warm hug, and mutter a gentle joke of a shared memory. Just like that, the spell of silence is broken. Other colleagues, inspired by this courageous act, begin to join in, chipping away at the awkwardness with heartfelt messages of support.

Instances like 'Remember that time we ordered pizza to the office at 11 pm?' prompt chuckles that transform the stifling silence to unexpected warmth.

The question, however, remains.

What would happen if that outlier hadn't taken the initiative to break the bystander effect? How sure are we that the people around us will protect us when we are expelled from the group? Is safety in numbers dependent on the existence of an outlier to open the floodgates of empathy and care? And if belonging can induce a state of frightening apathy, how can we challenge our own wiring to do better?

Step forward, offer a smile, and remind them that in the end it's the connections we build that truly matter—job or no job.

A few years ago, my mother was doing her weekly supermarket run at the local shopping centre. It is the same shopping centre she has been going to for over twenty years—a place of familiar faces and warm greetings. That day, sporting her comfy pair of sneakers and activewear, she made her way through the supermarket aisles. After buying what she needed for the week, she headed back to the car park to unload her groceries. It was a busy weekday afternoon and the car park was filled with cars and people.

As she was walking back to her car after returning her trolley, she felt the front of her shoe meet the edge of something raised on the ground. Next thing she knew, she had tripped and had fallen face first onto the gravel road.

Pain. Severe pain. So much pain that she laid there for a few seconds to gather her senses. As she slowly found the strength to push herself back up, she noticed that her face was bleeding. Covering her face in embarrassment, she hobbled back to her car. Onlookers watched from a distance, people gasped, but no one even half-heartedly offered to help. What originally felt like the warmth of the whole suburb surrounding her, suddenly felt like complete aloneness.

I will always remember her shaken tone when she called me. She never calls while I'm working, so I knew something was wrong. She told me that after stumbling back to her car, she realized the fall had snapped her two front teeth.

'I'm in a lot of pain, so I'm going to sit here for a while before I drive home,' she told me. Even though the logical side of my brain moved forward with solutions, I was confused and angry that no one had come to her aid. It was our small neighbourhood shopping centre in the suburbs of Sydney. It was a community of what I thought were caring people, who looked out for one another.

Fast forward a few years, I was walking out of the same shopping centre with my partner. From a distance, we saw an old man reversing his car. Around him were people and cars making way so he could manoeuvre out. But as he reversed, his car got closer and closer and . . . BANG!

It hit one of the parked cars on the side.

My partner and I both gasped, as did the other witnesses—some standing right next to his car. The old man then put his car into drive and slowly departed. Even though we were too far to verify the severity of the damage, the dent he had shoved in the car behind him seemed to have bounced back in some time. *Oh, it must be okay then*, I thought to myself.

I looked around at the other people who had seen the incident: no one seemed to be doing anything. *Oh well*, I thought, and I was ready to continue our day like nothing happened.

It was only when I saw the look of shock and horror on my partner's face that I questioned my behaviour. He burst out, 'I can't believe no one did anything! I was about to run over, but you didn't seem bothered and no one else moved!'

Oh no, I realized. *Maybe this is what happened the day when my mom fell.*

When there was no clear protocol or chain of command, when responsibility was dispersed across many, no one felt compelled to act. Moreover, this inaction also carried no guilt, because no one else did anything. In some strange, twisted way, it felt more *right* to do nothing.

And just like that, I was now guilty—of the same thing I had held a grudge against those who hadn't helped my mom that day.

It's scary to think how a concept so logical like safety in numbers can be so misleading. When we seek protection and belonging in times of vulnerability, 'safety in numbers' becomes more of a 'safety in silence', as everyone looks to each other for a cue on how to respond. Sadly, more often than not, no response ends up being the most common result.

Regardless of whether it is a life-threatening situation among familiar neighbours, a painful separation like layoff, or an injured fellow citizen in a small community, we're all likely to live in the illusion of safety in numbers, while simultaneously being the bystander when others need help. It calls to question the relationship between belonging and safety.

So, if safety in numbers is no guarantee, is there anything we can do to look after ourselves?

Yes—you're in luck.

The next time you get swept away by the comfort and safety of belonging, and such an emergency arises, remember: If people fail to act because of a diffusion of responsibility, then the only way to get them to act is to directly allocate it. In short, create an outlier in a sea of conformists.

So, if you find yourself in a situation where the community is unresponsive in providing the support you need, instead of drowning in your sorrows, make eye contact with someone, point at them, and give them direct instructions.

'You, in the red shirt! I need an ambulance. Call now!'

Such a call removes the lack of guilt as passive bystanders, because now, if they fail to act, they would be wilfully ignoring a plea for help that was specifically directed to them, not a general request to the group. This spotlighting of one person in the group will likely break the bystander effect: By doing so, you have effectively manufactured an outlier who will now move others to join the crusade.

The next time you find yourself on the sidelines, gripped by the inertia of the bystander effect, remember: You have a choice. You can be part of the passive crowd, or you can take the initiative and act.

Push beyond the comfort of doing nothing. Imagine if that person in need were your friend, your grandmother, your child, would you pin your hopes on someone else? Your voice, action, and courage aren't just responses; they're the sparks that break the spell of indifference.

REFLECTING

When we belong to a group, we feel protected. However, while it may feel safe to be surrounded by people, the bystander effect shows that the more people there are around you, the less likely someone will jump in to help you in the case of an emergency. The dispersed responsibility means people will turn to each other for an indication on how to behave, often resulting in no action.

Outliers have the power to break the bystander effect. If a brave outlier acts while others remain passive, their action is likely to move more people into action. If we are the person in need of help, we can also interrupt the bystander effect by looking a single person in the eye and giving them clear directions. 'You! Red shirt. Call the police!'

Ponder

- When was a time I needed help but no one came to my aid?
- When should I have spoken up or helped someone, but didn't? What were the thoughts that held me back?
- Who have I seen be a brave outlier? What did they do?

Be Your Own Self Coach

Social learning theory shows that we learn by observing and imitating the actions of others. We do much of it unknowingly, picking up behaviours that help us fit into the norms of society. Now that we are conscious of it, let's use it as a tool to stretch beyond what we've known.

Bring up that time when you encountered a brave outlier amid the crowd of conformists. How were people feeling before the outlier acted? Notice what shifted in people when they took action. Sink into that experience, the characters, the expressions, sensing their emotions and make visible the unspoken. Step out of yourself and circle above the scene. What do you notice from here?

Now float toward the outlier and step into them, assuming all their senses, thoughts and feelings. Seeing what they saw, hearing what they heard, feeling what they felt. What do you notice now?

Chapter 2.2 – The Power of Perception

Our quest for belonging extends beyond safety in numbers. Studies have shown that feeling a sense of belonging has profound effects on our well-being. Whether it is acceptance in a tight-knit social circle, settling into our space in a corporate hierarchy, or bonding with a community of like-minded individuals, when we find our place in a group, we experience a surge of positive emotions.

When we feel included and supported, our self-esteem boosts, our stress levels decrease, and we feel steadier in tackling the turbulence of what arises.

Why is this though?

Is there a magical energetic exchange between members of a group that tops up our life force? How is it that some people seem to flourish in the quiet of their own company, while others feel alive only in bustling crowds? How much of the benefits of belonging are directly attributed to social connection, and how much of it is in our own heads?

Psychologist Sheldon Cohen and his colleagues explored this relationship between social support and well-being.[8] While some supported the buffering model—suggesting that social support shields us and mitigates the impact of stressful events—others, however, took on the broader view that irrespective of timing, social support has a positive impact on our well-being.

Central to their argument is the measure of *perceived* social support—an individual's *belief* that they are cared for and have access to help—which has profound psychological and physiological benefits. The key word here is 'perceived'. That's right: Most research on the buffering effect measures *perceived* support, not *actual* support.

For example, someone who undergoes a highly stressful event may be buffered from its intensity if they *believe* they belong to a strong community of support. Conversely, a socially supported person could experience immense emotional strain if they interpreted an everyday situation as an acute stressor, believing they are alone and have no capability to deal with it.

The importance of this? We are more in control of our well-being than we think.

Are we social animals? Yes.

Does belonging to a network of support enhance our well-being? Also yes.

Can we boost our well-being by changing how we perceive the support we have? Absolutely. We have the power to create the benefits of belonging by reframing the narratives we tell ourselves. Reversely, we can live life as a stress-ball, surrounded by support but trapped in a narrative of misery.

Imagine John and Jordan at work. They work the same job, in the same company, in the same department, with the same boss. Their workload is the same, as is their capability. They even started on the same day: Monday, last week.

The only difference is, John is in the country alone, as he moved from overseas to start this job. His family will follow in the coming months; however, for now, he is all by himself in a strange new land. Jordan, on the other hand, grew up here. He lives in close proximity to his family and spends Saturdays playing badminton with his friends from NS—National Service, Singapore's mandatory military service.

While it may appear that John and Jordan are running on parallel tracks at the workplace, they have stark differences in their level of perceived social support. John, alone in a new country, would likely perceive a lower level of support. Jordan, on the other hand, surrounded by loved ones, is likely to perceive a greater level. Even if neither of them activates their support network, logic would follow that Jordan is likely to have a greater buffer in stressful situations, meaning his stress response—cortisol levels—should return to baseline faster than John's.

Let's add a twist to this storyline.

What if John is someone whom people would describe as a die-hard optimist? He believes he will always land on his feet, and when faced with challenges, help will always appear—oftentimes from strangers he has never met. When asked about how supported he feels, 'Always!' is his quick answer, even when he is facing, what appears to be, extremely adverse circumstances.

Jordan, on the other hand, finds living near his family suffocating. Since he was a child, he has always felt the pressure to perform. He feels his parents only care about what *they* want him to do; never about what *he* wants for himself. He may even go as far as to say that his parents don't know who he truly is. He has lived his life working towards the five Cs—cash, car, condominium, country club, and credit card—because it was all he knew. Playing badminton on Saturdays is Jordan's way of fulfilling his duty as a friend. While he was close to his mates around thirty years ago, a lot has changed, and his relationship with them now revolves around bringing up the same old stories of NS over and over. Being surrounded by the burden of many expectations is the furthest from what he considers to be social support. He dreams of going on a long holiday by himself—away from everything that ties him down. But the pressure of being seen as unfilial or irresponsible holds him back.

Knowing what you know now, how do you think John and Jordan will react the next time a stressful event hits? What did you come to understand about *perceived* support? If social support is to some degree cognitively mediated, then it calls for us to awaken to the role we cast ourselves in our story of belonging.

If the physiological impact of stress is based on perception of social support, rather than actual social support, then it gives us a clue in how we can call back power to ourselves by shifting our view of our circumstances. We generalize and concoct stories to make meaning of our world—a necessary filter for the bombardment of information we receive each second. However, in our endless creation of compelling fiction, how many of them are created in service of our happiness and well-being?

Reversely, when do we replicate the same patterns of self-pity and victimization? Maybe you are suffering and stuck in a negative situation from which you have no easy way out. Before you launch into another mental loop, remember your power. You can be your own safe harbour. Belonging to a community that can positively lift you up is great, but without it, you have the power to take refuge in yourself.

A powerful coaching question I like to use is, 'What is the other version of this story?' If we grow more aware of the stories we tell ourselves, we can reshape the fictions of low social support, low belonging, and replace them with more useful ones.

If you're reading this thinking, 'How does that differ to lying to yourself?', consider this: What is reality? What is the role that perception plays in reality? Or, perhaps, what is reality, if not perception?

The malleability of our reality comes from the flexibility of our mind, and our willingness to dismantle beliefs in curious exploration of new ones.

Let's give it a go.

Take a deep breath and evoke your curious self. Like in the movie *Inside Out* (2015), let's work with some of our emotions.

Invite your emotion of Curiosity to step forward. Now, ask Curiosity to bring up your network of social support: your colleagues, friends, family—anyone else you can think of. Next, give each network of support a score out of ten.

Time to invite another emotion: Envy. It can stand next to Curiosity; we're all great at accessing Envy, so this will be easy. Now, think about that person who has way *more* social support than you. Think about their robust networks of support, scoring theirs out of ten. Thanks, Envy.

Let's invite Empathy to take her place. As you see Curiosity and Empathy take the stage, bring up a person with very little or no social support. Look at them in the eye, see what they see, feel what they feel, and hear what they hear. Feel their aloneness, sense their sadness, and connect with their fear. What score of social support would you give them?

Now, looking back at your rating, how do you feel about your level of social support now? What did you notice? What learning have you gained about perception?

Well done. You would have realized from this exercise that our perceptions shift easily depending on the emotion we overlay on the situation. You may have also noticed how resourceful we are in evoking different emotions. We all have an emotional memory bank, and the ability to call on emotions we'd like to evoke.

Maybe you did it easily, maybe it took a bit more work, but we can all do it. Trace back to the last time you felt joy—real, full-hearted joy. Give yourself some time to sink back into that moment: notice your surroundings, the colours, the feel of the air. Take a snapshot of that moment and put it in your pocket. It's there now, right with you, whenever you want to access it. Maybe you can give this memory a shape and colour to anchor it. Anytime you want to retrieve it from your pocket, start with recalling that shape and colour.

The level of support we experience is as much shaped by our mind as by the people around us. It isn't just anything we receive, but something we can summon within ourselves. By intentionally evoking feelings and perceptions that support our well-being, we can experience the benefits of support without waiting for people to provide it.

So, next time you're feeling under the pump, go back to that anchored memory in your pocket. Remember what Curiosity, Envy, and Empathy showed you. We are used to imposing a certitude on the world, thinking that *our* truth is *the* whole truth, when it is a mere fragment of infinite realities.

Where do your stories lie on the harmful-healthy spectrum? What does one notch healthier look and feel like? What helps you shift in that direction?

If we want to wait until we have the perfect amount of social support to reap its benefits, we might find ourselves waiting for a long time. However, if we instead choose to take the reins in authoring our own lives, we have every power to create our own shelter in the storms of life. By tuning into our tool of perspective, we free ourselves from the obsession of needing to fit perfectly into the world.

Belonging to a strong network of support is also no guarantee of well-being, as perceived adequacy of support is what truly matters. The deep messages we internalize—such as we are uncared for, incapable, and helpless—will cripple us. They will paint the scenes of each day with misery and gloom, but regardless of where we are, a different perspective is only a thought away.

Like any unfit person who has just started a gym routine, we have an understanding that the distance between where we are today and our future dream body is not a bridge that can be crossed in a day. A sweaty workout session may feel great; however, when we look in the mirror, we probably look the same as yesterday. We put in a workout again, probably still looking the same. However, slowly, but surely, we know that if we keep going, something will change. Our legs may start to feel stronger; we may feel capable to run for a little bit longer. That exercise we feared like the plague somehow gets more manageable. The terrifying thought of running a half-marathon suddenly feels more achievable as our fitness level increases.

Here is the funny thing: We seem to have a completely different way of thinking about mental fitness. We download a meditation app and expect it to turn us into a zen master after listening to the first ten minutes. We feel frustrated noticing our flurry of thoughts and our inability to manage them. We rule out meditation forever, declaring that *it doesn't work*.

All in ten minutes!

Our attachment to the physical world means that we can accept the formation of muscle or building of endurance to be a process, and yet, with something intangible such as the mind, there seems to be an expectation that it should work like the flicking on and off of a switch.

News flash! Mental gym works like a physical one. Just like building muscle, shifting of perceptions is cultivated through practice and awareness. We all have mental shortcuts—our habitual thoughts and emotions—that are similar to a well-trodden path. We take these paths when we run on autopilot.

Think of walking home from the bus stop. Your mind can be somewhere else completely; however, your body will naturally walk you home. Or that moment you wake up after a night out, and before the headache hits you, you are pleasantly surprised at how, somehow, you managed to get home—even though you have no recollection of it. Many of these well-trodden paths are in place to get us through life—just like getting us home after a drunken night—however, if there is a road that continually leads us to suffering, snap yourself out of autopilot. Reroute before it steers you off the course!

Slipping up is normal, so is accepting the reemergence of habitual perceptions. But instead of letting them consume you, mentally shake yourself awake. I find it useful to have fun with it by saying 'STOP!' out loud, catching my unwanted habit as if to say, 'Hey you! I see you!' In doing so, I nudge myself, while offering unexpected shock and entertainment for those around—all while reframing and reorienting my thinking.

We are powerfully resourceful, and the benefits of social support are accessible to us right away. There is no need to wait until we are in a place of perfect belonging before we can enjoy it.

REFLECTING

We can bring about the benefits of belonging through manoeuvring our perception. The placebo effect, where we can 'think' ourselves well or sick, shows the power of our thoughts in signalling responses in our body. Our mind is like our CEO. Every time someone does something that makes us go, 'What the heck was that idiot doing?', we signal our body to release the chemicals of annoyance and frustration. Alternatively, if the same event happens and we tell ourselves, 'How interesting! I wonder how he arrived at that conclusion,' we nudge it to create feelings of curiosity.

Same event—different chemical responses.

Psychologists have shown that our perceived adequacy of support can influence our ability to cope with stress—more so than the actual availability of support. Hence, we can elevate our wellbeing through changing our perception.

Ponder

- What factors play into shaping my perception of belonging and social support?
- What would be useful to remind myself of in times of stress?
- How would someone with high levels of social support think and feel? What are examples of their internal dialogue?

Be Your Own Self Coach

Often, if we can get beyond the immediacy of our own experience, we begin to realize the richness of our resources. Find a quiet and comfortable place where you can sit undisturbed. Take a few deep breaths to centre yourself. Know that you are in your own sanctuary, where you are safe and supported. Begin to visualize your inner self as a cozy home. See the colours of the walls, smell the scent of the flowers, associate with the feelings of that home. Immerse fully in the richness of this moment.

Write down five core components you imagined in this house.

What resources do they represent? What values do they honour? Notice yourself expand as you add more and more into your beautiful house. Walk around the house, uncover the unique treasures of this house that makes it like no other, admire the magnificence that is you.

How do you feel now about the resources available to you? What has come to your awareness about social support and belonging?

Chapter 2.3 – Harmony and Tension

Family is a place many think of when we bring up belonging. For some because they truly feel it, for others, because it feels like the 'right' answer, or for those that don't say family, but feel the ache of its absence.

In Asia, harmony is one of the indicators of belonging. When interactions feel smooth and conflict-free, it suggests that people feel secure, accepted, and connected to one another. Tension, on the other hand, hints that things are not going well. It can be read as a sign that relationships are fragile and that someone may not fully fit.

Let's peer a little deeper into this dynamic, where harmony, legacy, and face are often paramount. It doesn't take many conversations to realize that the seemingly cohesive appearance often comes with an undercurrent of unspoken tension: an invisible weight, and strung onto it is the expectation to perform, conform, and preserve peace for the sake of the collective, even at the cost of emotional honesty.

In my recent conversation with university students, when asked what made them pick the course they were studying, a sea of blank expressions and awkward giggles came as response, followed by one quiet voice: 'Because my parents told me to'.

'Get good grades, so you can make your parents proud,' I heard an announcement at a high school assembly.

Obedience is an expression of filial piety. Rooted in ideals that emphasize respect for elders, family unity, and close bonds.

In many Asian families, there is a deep-seated desire to avoid conflict and maintain the façade of harmony.

As someone who was born in Taiwan, grew up in Thailand and Australia, and spent most of my adulthood in Singapore, harmony perplexed me. Depending on where I was, it was either encouraged, seen as an absolute necessity, or rarely mentioned.

I remember asking my teacher in primary school why, a classmate, who had been throwing a tantrum, was allowed to stay in class even though he was disrupting the rest of us. Quickly, I was hushed into silence, told my question was inappropriate, and that we must be more considerate and tolerant. No explanation—just accept it and move on.

One of the funny things I learned about the Chinese culture is that when invited for tea, **進來喝茶** ('jìn lái hē chá'), there is a significant possibility that they don't actually want you to accept. There is an unspoken expectation that you will decline profusely, after which they will continue to insist. Then, after going back and forth for some time, the conversation abruptly ends, and you leave.

One time, I happily accepted an invitation, only to have them suggest that it was getting late and some other time would be better. Then, with a nod and awkward smile, I watched the door begin to close on my face. It was utterly confusing! However, I later learned that **進來喝茶** ('jìn lái hē chá') is more of a polite passing comment than a real invitation.

Another fun one: If you bump into a friend on the street, you should have a long list of compliments prepared—regardless of how far they are from the truth. If they are with their children, the praises should include how smart, obedient, or good-looking they are. I spent the first eighteen years of my life believing that I must be some kind of supermodel. Every time we met my parents' friends, they would say, '**你女兒好漂亮**' ('nǐ nǚ'ér hǎo piào liàng') meaning 'Your daughter is so pretty.' It's often paired with an overexaggerated look, as if they've just discovered the eighth wonder of the world. It was only long after my teens that I realized it's the standard compliment used for everyone. Looking back at photos of my pimply face, gothic-make up, and questionable outfits, I am impressed how they even managed the words out of their mouth.

Coming back to the family context.

The need for harmony means that many topics are still out-of-bounds in certain families. Invariably, there is a spectrum of family dynamics, so what I'm sharing is a combination of what I have witnessed and experienced across Asia. To preserve peace and avoid discomfort, topics about mental health, personal struggles, or negative deviations—that fall outside what is respectable—are often sidelined. Playing happy family is a sign of respect for the elders. Even when there are issues between family members, the preference is to opt for indirect spokespeople: for example, one aunt asking another to speak to the concerned person—yet never addressing it with them directly.

In coaching leaders across Asia, 'living up to expectations' has been a prevalent theme. As children, many were conditioned to obey, study hard, and exceed academically. It was a way to earn validation, a quiet proof that they were worthy. As adults, many continued to follow the well-trodden path, sticking to careers and life trajectories that never felt quite right. It was all about carrying the burden of other people's expectations, while comforting themselves by calling it maturity.

Over time, resentment builds and they feel increasingly disconnected from themselves—all the while the family charade goes on. Unwillingness to participate in this show may be seen as a lack of respect or selfishness, of prioritizing oneself over the group.

In my twenties, I learned about the term **剩女** ('shèng nǚ') literally meaning 'leftover woman'—used for unmarried women in their late-twenties or older. It describes a woman who has apparently passed her prime and now supposedly holds less value on the marriage 'market'. At that time, living in Shanghai, someone referred to me with it after I had turned thirty and was still single. I found it rather hilarious. I thought my friend was being sarcastic, so I proudly donned the title, introducing myself with it to everyone I met.

In openly bringing up this 'leftover woman' as a topic of conversation, I came to learn how real this pressure was for many young women. The magnitude of anxiety they faced while attending family gatherings or direct parental pressure was disturbing to witness. One even confided in me her fear of being disowned if she didn't get married soon.

Similarly, the celebratory topics you bring to the table—your shining grades, your salary increase, or your progression in attaining the five Cs—all bring pride to your family. 'Your parents are the happiest when you do well,' I was told, 'So, you must work hard, because you must do it for your family.'

Depending on your family dynamics, some of this may feel archaic and outdated; however for many, this mentality is as alive as ever. The pride and honour of belonging to a family can carry an unhealthy weight of expectation that stifles genuine connection. The aim of harmony in fostering togetherness often results in dissonance between what is seen and what is experienced: A façade of laughter and smiles, hiding feelings of emotional isolation as we feel that only our positive parts are deserving of recognition.

This avoidance of difficult conversations creates a breeding ground for unresolved tension. This unspoken field of unmet expectations manifests with snide remarks like, 'It's so nice that your friend Julie has her husband to look after her,' to the unmarried daughter or 'Look at Kenneth; he is already in medical school,' to the son who has yet to figure out what he wants to do in life.

When indirect ways of communicating disappointment—masked as encouragement—overtake open dialogue, we are left to navigate our feelings alone, fostering a perpetual drive to seek approval, never feeling good enough, and only speaking out when we have resolved our own problem.

Instead of using this underlying tension as fertile soil to grow together, it is tucked away into the darkness and left unhealed and unaddressed. Family gatherings begin to feel more ritualistic or duty-driven, held together by the authority of elders rather than a natural coming together of people who seek to deepen their connection with one another. Interactions play out like well-rehearsed theatre. Love is expressed through criticism or financial support—but never articulated in words. Individuals seek out their own methods of healing from this trauma, for if it were raised to the family, it may be faced with defensiveness, or be considered shameful and unfilial 不孝 ('bù xiào'). While there is merit in harmonious belonging, it does not equate to feigning happy family while dodging the real issues underneath.

As mentioned, this by no means is a generalization of all families. However, it provokes us to consider what it really means when we say we belong to our family: Do we say it out of a sense of respect, duty, or filial responsibility? All because of bloodline or last name? Is there really a depth of authentic connection and acceptance, where we are embraced fully as our weird and wonderful selves? Or is there something we need to wake up to—something to be nurtured within the underlying tension?

Gordon comes from a Thai Chinese family. Having been sent to boarding school in London at the age of ten, much of his family's traditions were foreign to him. Having spent most of his childhood studying overseas, he felt a greater sense of belonging to his friends than to his family. His parents are devoted Christians, and as someone who lived away from that community, he found the intensity of their faith overbearing.

His excitement to see his parents during his holidays was shadowed by the pressure he felt for being atheist. 'The first day [being with family] was usually good, but by the second or third day, the preaching would begin,' he said. An unspoken distance developed between him and his parents as he felt constantly shamed for not being Christian. One of his most painful memories is of the time his father told him that he would go to hell if he did not follow Jesus.

He grew up to have a very unhealthy relationship with his parents. The more they preached, the less he wanted anything to do with them and Christianity. He found excuses to stay away, grappling with the guilt of feeling like a bad son while knowing that any interaction would result in the worsening of their relationship. It was while completing his post-graduate studies, he became severely depressed.

One day, when he went to the mental health centre at school, the practitioner he spoke with noticed the severity of his condition and called the police. He was handcuffed and taken to hospital. There, within the white walls of his ward, were the most harrowing days of his life. 'It was like I had taken on the suffering of everyone in that hospital', he described. The pain struck him with such intensity that he wanted everything to end.

Though, looking back now, while the hospital was terrifying, 'It also saved my life,' he said. 'My fear of failing suicide kept me from attempting it. I was scared that if I tried and failed, I would have to stay there for longer.'

When his parents were informed about this episode, the doctor stressed the importance of his need for safety, love, care, and non-judgemental space. When they came to pick him up, he was still fragile, though grateful to be going home. At this point, he said, his parents hadn't fully understood the severity of his condition. 'I felt they were still taking it lightly,' he confessed.

Even though his parents had little idea that their judgement was a major trigger for him, they just wanted their son to be well. Soon after his return, at dinner with friends, his parents started bringing up his drinking habit, saying he lost his way because he was hanging with the wrong crowd. By this, they meant those who had steered him away from the Christian faith. Every cell in his body moved into fight-or-flight mode. He wanted to run. He wanted to escape to as far as he could get.

At that point, there was nothing about his family that he felt he belonged to. Aside from sharing a last name, his feelings of forever falling short of their expectations led him to retreat completely. His parents were unable to understand why, and put it down to the depression. No longer feeling that he had anything in common with the people he was supposed to belong to, his condition spiralled to rock bottom.

But just as it seemed like it was reaching a point of no return, something shifted.

Unlike the emotional avoidance or absence of communication we might be used to seeing, Gordon's family had a different relationship with tension. When they finally realized how serious the situation was, instead of perpetuating it through denial or burying him with more life advice, they spoke about the discomfort together. 'It was so hard' Gordon said, 'because I never told them about how I really felt. It also made it extra frustrating because my mum would get super defensive and my dad would have sudden memory loss and have no recollection of events. But what held it together was our commitment to sit with each other in the mud.

Facing the uncomfortable truth of their crumbled relationship was what saved it. Instead of seeing the broken parts of their relationship as signs of failure, they saw it as the gateway to strengthening their bond. 'We stayed with each other. We sat with each other. Even if there was an outburst and we walked away, we came back to talk about what happened. We made it a point to highlight with each other at the end of each conversation how we have grown together.'

Whenever they felt any strain or tension arise, they would bravely inch towards it. If something didn't feel right, their instinctive response became disclosure and discussion. Every tense, conversation was defined as progress, and every disagreement celebrated as a deepening of their relationship. 'We became mirrors for each other,' he said. Soon, they were reflecting aspects of one another's unchecked selves back at each other and addressing them together. Though harmony was a rare occurrence, these rough seas became their greatest strength, bringing them together where others usually drift apart.

It has been over ten years now, and they are still on that journey today. It was through this process that Gordon started to understand his own relationship with God. Born from a place of love, rather than obligation, he started to accept God into his life, at his own time and pace. He also recognized that his dependence on his parents for self-worth and acceptance had been hindering him from being able to interact with them from a place of gratitude.

When we misidentify belonging as a person or place that can complete us, we sacrifice the potential for real connection. We consume our energy trying to ensure things go the way they should, and that people keep making us feel the way we should feel. Confined to a narrow world of *this should* and *that shouldn't*, while closing ourselves off from the wholeness that is our natural being, we end up caging ourselves in an illusion of clarity, disabling our curiosity to learn—all the while navigating an inherently ambiguous world.

It's time for us to rethink our relationship with harmony, starting with our families. Our formative years are critical to the development of our psyche, so the relationships we breed at home seep into our adult lives. We may love our family with all our heart, but if the rawness of life's rollercoaster is expected to be experienced alone, can we really call it a place of belonging?

For the happiness of our parents, we can contort ourselves to the point we forget who we are. Traditions that forbid scrutiny are not sacred but stagnant. And while unchallenged traditions offer the comfort of familiarity, it suffocates dialogue and creates separation. Do the traditions we engage in support the fostering of a stronger bond? When we experience tension, do we see it as fertile soil or root rot?

We have two alternatives: We may take the easy route of accepting things the way they are, or we may begin to move the dial to extend beyond our known realities. Remember: The richness of belonging emerges from embracing tension. While harmony is a comforting façade, it silences the very part of us that needs expression. The richness of belonging can often be found in tension itself, for it pushes us to confront hard truths, such as realizing when we have misplaced our self-worth in the approval of others.

Tension, is a signal pointing us towards a deeper dimension of belonging. It is in times of discomfort, doubt, or conflict that we are invited to shake the foundations of façade. It peels back the layers of expectation, conditioning, and harmony to question where we truly stand with others, and more importantly, with ourselves. It is the roar of our intuition, urging us to pause, reflect, and realign. Through this process, tension becomes the catalyst for growth: with others, our relationships have the chance to become more authentic; with ourselves, guiding us to ask the hard questions that awaken our inner wisdom. It is here that we experience real connection: not as something we must earn, but a natural unfolding that comes with being fully present with ourselves and the world around us.

For Gordon, this came with finding his own relationship with God. For you, it may be something else. As Eckhart Tolle mentioned in his book, *The Power of Now*, the word 'God' has been so regularly misused, it has become a closed concept.[9] So whether you call it God, the universe, your intuition, your North Star, your purpose, you can use any term to capture the aliveness that brings you home to yourself.

How can we achieve this though, if unlike Gordon's family, our willingness to embrace tension is not shared by those we wish to grow with? What is one to do, if our encouragement of others to move towards tension is repeatedly faced with push back and disdain?

Here's a thought. Sometimes, when we learn something new, we get excited to share it and bring others onboard. We do it with an intensity of enthusiasm that is received as pushy or forceful. We insist that they *should* embrace it with us—sometimes judging them if they don't. We blame *our* problems on *their* unwillingness—focusing all our attention on them, and none on ourselves. We've likely been on the receiving end too, feeling pressured to support an idea or product a friend is passionately promoting.

Now compare that with the empathy of knowing that we all struggle with big feelings and have our own timing. Tension is uncomfortable and our instinct is to reject it. So forcing it on them is like expecting a baby to enjoy the terrible tasting cough medicine. An adult who understands the value of a cough medicine would willingly take it, however, a baby who neither has the understanding nor desire, would respond very differently.

There is a difference between effecting change through lack, or through love. Lack is ego-driven, judgemental, and insistent.

Love, on the other hand, is open, compassionate, and free from expectation. When we try to move hearts, to ignite bravery, we will only succeed when we come from a place of love—and we often try to fool ourselves into believing that our lack is love.

Take, for example, a strict parent who demands respect. They tell themselves it comes from a place of love, to direct their child towards making the right life choices. However, behind what they label as love lies a deep fear that if the child makes their own decisions, they might be unable to protect them from the consequences, thus losing control. While there is no denying that a parent *loves* their child, the actions driven from that love is that of grasping love—driven by fear and lack, clinging to who they think the child should be, rather than embracing who they already are in their wholeness.

Contrast this with a parent who trusts in their child's journey. They set boundaries where needed but also allow space for mistakes, exploration, and individuality. Their love is not a leash but a foundation—a steady presence that says, 'You are enough, just as you are, and I trust you to grow into who you are meant to be.'

Reflect on your own experiences. When have you tried to guide someone towards a journey you see for them, without noticing that your intentions might feel like control? What would coming from a place of love look like? If you've moved towards tension from a place of love, it shouldn't matter how they respond as love is in service of the person you offer it to.

We can extend our arms out to those whom we wish to grow with. However, they are on their own journey, with their own timing and readiness. The biggest mistake is to impose growth on someone who is neither ready, nor has the will. You cannot wake someone who is pretending to sleep. Nor do we have the authority to judge someone else's readiness.

We may long to guide people, especially when we are excited to go through the journey ourselves. However, each person's evolution is personal, it's called 'personal development' for a reason, and our own journeys would lose meaning if it were dependent on someone coming along. Like a river, we all make our way on different types of boats, starting from different locations. Our end points are different, and depending on where we are, the roughness of our rides differ as well. So, who are we to say where someone else must be in life?

Moreover, it would be a grave disservice to ourselves if we buy into the excuse that we are incapable of doing the work without someone else doing it with us. The best chance we have in igniting the spirit of growth in another is through our own personal growth—to stay with our *own* tension, sit with our *own* discomfort, and to share our *own* learnings.

Remember the misconception about mental fitness: our expectation that it should work immediately? Don't expect this to be a smooth ride either. Staying with tension is more like stepping into a room that is both still and chaotic: a place where you suddenly feel everything. Tension can be mental and physical, and a good place to start is by noticing your physical tension. Take 10 minutes to be with yourself. No group chat meme banter, no music, and no TV in the background—just you. Feel the rise and fall of your chest as you breathe in and out.

We spend so much time in our heads that we rarely give our bodies the centre stage it deserves. As you breathe, notice the sensations in your body. Maybe your shoulders ache, your jaw clamps down, or there's a tightening of discomfort in your stomach you hadn't noticed before. Anytime an instinct urges you to get up and move, distract or numb yourself, bring yourself back and stay with your tension.

Breathe into the tightness, observe the discomfort, and connect with it. The longer you stay, the more you notice. Tension isn't random: it has stories to tell, it's the memories stored in the body, the trapped energy you may have pushed away. Every sensation is a signal, and every signal carries with it a message. Thank the tension for revealing itself to you. Sit, stay, and learn from it. Soften the discomfort with each exhale, letting it move through you instead of fighting or confining it.

Soon, you'll realize—through experience—that tension was never the enemy, but the nudge, inviting you to reconnect with yourself, to release the emotional burden you have been carrying. Over time, this practice becomes a quiet, portable strength for you to take with yourself anywhere you go—a way to turn inwards with presence and compassion, even when waters are rough. It's not about fixing or escaping, but *being*.

Did you realize what you just experienced?

You are doing the very thing Gordon practiced with his family, but you've started with yourself—a transformation from the inside out. Each moment you stay with your own tension, you open more and more to the essence of your being. If people are willing to grow alongside you, it's a gift to relish. But if not, do not place your power in their hands; your journey doesn't depend on their willingness. Homecoming begins when we belong to ourselves, and we can start right where we are.

When we train to be steadfast with ourselves, we begin to tune into a wisdom that is beyond what any culture, tradition, or elder could teach us. If we shrink into silencing ourselves to preserve a false sense of belonging, we starve our authenticity and create separation. True belonging doesn't require harmony, and healthy conflict doesn't destroy it. Let life all the way in, reach into the ugliness, and transmute it into strength. Tension is the doorway back to our aliveness.

REFLECTING

We mislabel harmony as a sign of belonging and tension as a sign of separation. This prioritization of harmony can result in emotional isolation where individuals feel the need to only exhibit the parts of themselves they consider are acceptable. However, tension can be the nurturing ground for growth, but only if we learn to face it and stay with it.

When we do this collectively, holding non-judgemental space to sit with discomfort, our growth can be stimulated by the growth of others, and we can be mirrors for each other's unchecked selves. However, the journey of self-growth can be equally rewarding. Our willingness to reveal to ourselves our vulnerabilities, and to stay with it, will inspire others to embark on their journey.

Ponder

- What do you believe about watching, observing and being aware?
- What you resist, persists. What have you been resisting?
- Did you know that excitement and anxiety have similar physiological underpinnings? They both lead to the release of hormones like adrenaline, cause increased heart rate, and heightened alertness. The key difference being how we label it. How would you like to relabel tension?

Be Your Own Self Coach

To move beyond our tension and suffering, we must courageously dig it up and examine it without judgement. The garden of our hearts cannot flourish without working through the weeds. This is an exercise where we go further than observing our emotions by communicating with them.

Trace back your timeline and bring up an event that felt tense and uncomfortable. If you're doing this for the first time, you can start with a mild tension that's easier to face. Associate with that experience-feeling, seeing and hearing what you felt. Now identify where that feeling is in your body, represent it: weight, size, colour, and texture. Bring it forward and outside of you, until you can see it in front of you.

Now, we are going to invite the emotion to communicate by personifying it. Have a conversation with it, using the following questions as a guide. The focus is to tune into the emotion. The questions are to help you start a conversation.

- What is your highest intention for me?
- What do you want me to know?
- How can I integrate your wisdom into my life?

Beyonding

Be Your Own Detective

We grow more aware each time we write out our thoughts and feelings. Let your intuition guide you as you complete these statements.

Belonging to a group brings ....

Safety in numbers only exists when ....

If I rely on the group to feel safe, then ....

When I feel stressed I ....

The story I tell myself about support is ....

It would help if I reminded myself that...................................

I feel calmer when I believe that ....

My dad thinks that harmony is ....

When there is tension my mom ....

The toughest relationship I worked through was ....

That relationship allowed me to ....

A mantra I'd like to gift myself is...

Send these statements to a friend. You can reflect separately or compare responses and grow together.

Chapter 3

TIGHTROPE

When we are immersed in a place of belonging, it feels strong, solid, and immovable. Yet, it couldn't be further from the truth.

We find comfort in believing that things are stable, when, in fact, everything around us is constantly changing. The apple on the table is decaying before our eyes—though our mind blocks out that reality. When we bite into it, we don't think think to ourselves 'I'm eating a decaying apple.' Instead, we believe it is the same apple we had bought four hours ago. We have a way of censoring out what is indiscernible to the human eye, and this bias of permanence leads us to misplace our eggs in shaky baskets.

Like harmony and tension, the idea of permanence lulls us into a sense of ease. But the discomfort of facing our mental falsehoods is how we pierce through the illusions of the mind. 'I know who I am,' we like to declare, as if the self were a solid statue carved in stone. 'This is what they *should* do,' as if the tides and winds could be tamed by our certainties. The closer we cling to these notions, the more we trap ourselves in limited realities. Instead of struggling against uncertainty, what if we could reconnect with our natural fluidity?

Belonging is much more like a tightrope, after all.

Chapter 3.1 – Impermanence

I'm dying. We all are.

Time is the bank account we spend from, without ever knowing its true net balance. We're all simultaneously living and dying. Life is a constant state of becoming and unbecoming, and yet, it may shock you if someone were to tell you that they are dying. Perhaps, you would think they have fallen ill, or some big news is about to be shared.

This dance between our awareness and denial implies we choose to focus on the normalcy of being alive, while ignoring the truth of our mortality. It is not about pessimism, but examining the true nature of life and understanding what it does to us when we only choose to acknowledge part of it.

When someone is on their death bed, it's considered inappropriate to speak about that person's imminent death. Discussions about estates or even bringing up the word 'death' in conversation can be considered exceptionally rude, especially with an elder. The thought that by doing so, you are wishing for them to die, makes it difficult to get affairs in order, for risk of being seen as disrespectful or unfilial. This is ironic as it is the elder who has the knowledge to bring the estate together. One woman, whose mother had recently passed was asked by her father to say that her mother was travelling, if anyone ever asked about her in public.

Inspired by the book *The Tibetan Book of Living and Dying* by Sogyal Rinpoche, I once asked my mom if I could speak to my grandfather about death. He was well into his nineties, and it felt rather strange to me that we were all playing happy family, like he was going to live forever. I was curious about how he feels nearing death, if there was fear or confusion that comes with it. But there was no outlet for him to express himself, or for us to comfort him. Also, I thought, he could impart wisdom about life with us. My mom was quick to tell me that such a topic would not be welcomed, saying it would be hurtful and highly disrespectful. She is probably right, but it did get me wondering about why it's such a big no-no.

It's not about being frivolous about death, or dismissing it. Instead, it is about honouring the significance of death rather than deny its existence. There are libraries dedicated to pregnancy and childbirth. People jump to share their experiences with you the moment you mention you're pregnant. Everyone rushes in with a healthy dose of unsolicited advice to expecting parents. But the stage turns silent for those nearing death. The psychological support on dying, while already sparse, is often cloaked in euphemisms that make it vague and confusing.

One of the best trainings I have attended was from a local hospice. I was taught about how death works, the progressive fading of one's senses, and how our sense of touch is the last to go. I learned that even when people are no longer responsive, or are unable to see or hear you, they can still feel your touch—so, holding their hand can offer them great comfort.

They shared that many people are scared of dying or feel fear in their last moments. However, instead of tucking it away into the abyss of the unspoken, they encouraged open and compassionate communication about death: creating a space for the dying to express their feelings, allowing them to share their fears, offering assurance, and demystifying the process.

So, what's this got to do with belonging?

Like all things, our identities are fleeting as well. Every statement starting with 'I am . . .' or 'I belong to . . .' carries a certitude about what we are and our position in this world. It gives us the comfort to live in the falsehood that we are one clear thing, connected to other distinct, clear things. Yet, our belonging to cultures, communities, companies or even people operate in a constant state of flux.

We see this in parents who idolize their kids. They love them so intensely, it leads to overinvolvement, neglect of boundaries, and a suffocating level of control masked by what they believe as belonging with their kid—captured in the frame of 'I'm a good parent'. This grasping ends up damaging the relationship, as the child learns they are deserving of love only when they adhere to the wishes of their parents. If they're lucky, they may awaken to their own North Star, doing the difficult work of untangling themselves from the web of their parents' expectations. Or, they may continue to place their self-worth in their parents, until one day, when the guiding hand passes on, they are left facing a life they never truly chose.

We don't need to be fortune tellers to understand impermanence intellectually, but we have a deep emotional aversion to it. We learn about 'object permanence' when we are eight to twelve months old. Before eight months, psychologist Jean Piaget observed, infants often stop searching for toys once they become hidden from their view.[10] For example, if a toy was placed under a blanket, to the infant, the toy no longer exists. However, the cognitive shift at eight to twelve months means that infants would actively search for objects, even after they disappear from sight. We start to understand a continuity of existence, moving away from the simple here-and-now.

This understanding that things continue to exist, even when we can't see them, is a milestone in our cognitive development, and is essential for us to function effectively in the world. However, the psychological extension of this can entangle us in nostalgia, regret, or obsessive attachment to things that are no longer with us. We cling to what is no longer present: lost love, changed circumstances, the things we want, and those who've left us. We have a natural attachment to permanence, making it hard for us to fully ground ourselves in the present.

Our today is not really 'today', for it is burdened with the weight of all our yesterdays. Every connection of belonging we make, in turn, becomes that new toy we have caught sight of and never want to let go of. We close ourselves off to the freshness of new possibilities and resist the irrefutable truth that everything we have will, one day, leave us. Our desire for stability and security holds us in an illusion of a fixed reality, and within it, the presence of a fixed self.

We can't bear the thought that those we belong to might, one day, walk away from us and become strangers. The belonging we hold so fervently to our organizations or communities is subject to the ever-evolving dynamics of the people within it. Just like trying to grasp as much water as we can with our bare hands, we fight against the fluid flow of the world, because we wilfully blind ourselves to how it works. We believe there to be one clear 'me', who comes with fixed behaviours and ways of thinking. 'This is just me,' we say. 'People don't change,' we affirm. However, upon examining our thoughts, their coming and going is little more than clouds passing in the wind. Even a similar thought is never the exact same thought twice. Our emotions surge and fade, combine and collapse like waves meeting a shore.

We understand it from our logical mind when we see it happen to others. But somehow, we refuse to accept it as our own reality. The pain of change comes not from the change itself, but the refusal of the mind to accept that nothing ever stands still. Our seemingly solid identities separates us from the shapelessness of our being. It keeps us in confined realities, expending all our energy into trying to keep in place things that were never meant to stay together forever.

Our pride in belonging to cultures is built on a set of ideas handed down from others that guided us on how life should be lived. We defend traditions like our life depends on it, yet we treat similar second-hand information—hearsay, for example—with caution in a court of law, due to its inherent unreliability. Every piece of convincing information we encounter is reshaping, altering, and evolving our beliefs. The longer we stubbornly hold onto thoughts like 'It must be like this,' 'We just have to,' or 'It's always been done this way,' the more we struggle against the realm of possibility.

But what if we could curiously entice ourselves away from the narrowness of our mind? Pause, and ask yourself:

- Who am I beyond the roles I play, the titles I hold, or the names I've been given? When those are stripped away, what remains?
- Am I afraid of losing my sense of self, or am I afraid of discovering that nothing was ever as fixed as I thought?

If we bring our centre of gravity inwards and connect with the field of our being, we will realize that there were never any must-bes or should-dos. There was never a fixed place of belonging outside of us, but only a perennial unfolding, flow of aliveness within us, glowing with possibilities.

Even when it comes to our physical selves, we look at our bodies and definitely proclaim, 'This is me'. However, what part of it is 'me'? If we were to amputate an arm, would it still be 'me'? What if we had surgery and removed a kidney? How many of our arms, legs, and body parts would we need to exclude before 'me' stops being 'me'? Even without brutal imagery of amputation, the seemingly permanent body we see each day is never the same.

'No man ever steps into the same river twice, for the river is not the same river, and he is not the same man,' said Greek philosopher Heraclitus. Scientifically, we lose 50 to 70 billion cells every day in the natural process of cellular turnover. Skin cells are shed and renewed every two to four weeks, and blood cells every few months. My partner is constantly concerned by how much hair he finds of mine on the ground each day. Every seven to ten years, we belong to none of the physical parts of our body that had existed before—we are a whole new person. However, in our minds, we haven't changed. Aside from some extra wrinkles, longer hangovers, and slightly yellower teeth, our mind miraculously tricks us into believing that everything else has stayed the same.

Yet, the truth is, we never belong to anything forever, not even our physical selves. Like the Japanese concept of *wabi sabi*, which celebrates transience and imperfection, the natural cycle of growth and decay has a beauty in itself. Each time we attach ourselves to someone or somewhere, we deny that beauty and misplace our source of happiness.

Buddha referred to this as mistaking suffering for happiness, seeing the drug as relief when it is actually deepening our addiction. We create an expectation that our place of belonging is responsible for providing with us with healing, acceptance, and safety—we feel hurt and betrayed when they fall short. The partner that doesn't love us the way we want them to, the company that doesn't make us feel included: The fragility of these ideals imposes an unmeetable expectation that people and places *should* be what we want them to be, what we *need* them to be.

We live in a state of lack, feeling unfulfilled each time belonging fails to be the way it *should*, hindering us from being able to love and appreciate them the way they *are*. Instead of being the child who searches endlessly for a lost toy, what if we could relearn the ways of appreciating the here-and-now, enjoying each new toy as it appears, and letting go of the ones that vanish?

The demand for certainty and predictability is the losing hand at the casino called Life. If we could grow comfortable with the ever-evolving nature of our existence, we could redirect the energy back inwards that we channeled outside of us. Stay with the discomfort as you peel away your illusion of permanence. Remind yourself that nothing in the world really ever belongs to us, so there is nothing to be afraid of in letting go.

The tension may feel unbearable. But know as you keep letting go, there will come a point that you will find something of a very different nature. It is both stillness and movement, both power and peace—an everlasting, ever-existing aliveness that is your being. It comes with no labels, fixed shape, or characteristics. It is open and infinite, like the vastness of the sky. When we look to the sky, our attention is often drawn to what passes through it—the clouds, the rain, the thunder. We define it by what occupies it at that moment.

But when was the last time you became aware of the sky itself—the ever-present sky that exists behind all storms, clouds, rain and shine? The one that's constant and unchanging, holding space for everything that comes and goes. It has no fixed colour, shape, or form; yet, it remains untouched by the storms, undamaged by the fiercest weather. The sky is a reminder of impermanence: the transient nature of all things that appear and fade, held by something deeper and ever-present. Like the sky, our true nature is not defined by the passing storms of emotion, the clouds of thought, or the fleeting moments of sunshine in life. Beneath it all, there is an enduring presence within us—steady, vast, and unchanging—no matter what comes or goes.

We can remain stuck in the vicious cycle of seeking permanence, or we can gently loosen our grip, prepare ourselves for loss, reconnect with our being—knowing that before we belonged anywhere, we belonged to ourselves.

REFLECTING

In our journey of life, we oscillate between the joy of living and the reality of our mortality, often choosing to ignore the latter. To speak of death or departure feels painful and taboo yet we are all simultaneously living and dying, coming together and falling apart. We cling to identities and people, convinced of their permanence, yet they are transient. Nothing stays with us forever, even our bodies are changing moment by moment. Acceptance of this impermanence invites us to confront our attachments and expectations. There is an ever-present aliveness we connect to when we take the brave step of letting go of our delusions of permanence, relaxing into the natural rise and fall of life as it unfolds.

Ponder

- Recall a time when you resisted letting go, and how in hindsight it was signalling you towards a new experiences. What did you learn from this?
- What are the beautifully imperfect things in your life you love?
- How can acknowledging the fleeting nature of life inspire you to engage more fully in each moment?

Be Your Own Self Coach

People often think of meditation as the beautiful, peaceful practice of visualizing nature and stillness. While this may feel nice in the moment, the deep contemplative practice of meditation is about facing what's uncomfortable to cultivate awareness, compassion, and an enriched understanding of life. One of the most powerful meditations I've found is the meditation on death, which was taught to me by my teacher.

As you feel the rise and fall of your breath and sink into a meditative state, move through time to the day you are on your deathbed. Your friends and family are stood around your bed: look into their faces as they look down at yours, feel the light of their aliveness connect with yours. As you lose your sense of hearing, the words they say quieten as if they are speaking from a distance.

Slowly, you lose all sense of hearing, and your vision begins to fade. They are now blurrier and blurrier, fading away. You can feel the gentle touch of their hand on yours, but even that becomes more difficult to discern as your sense of touch starts to fade too. Feel the love you have for them, the gratitude you have for the life you lived. You want to hold on, but know that it's time to let go. Feel the comfort of knowing everything is as it should be, as you reflect on the impermanence of life. Hold that feeling and let that feeling be your object of meditation. Meditate on that feeling. Get familiar with it, understand it, let it teach you.

Notice now what happens to the old strength of attachments you once had to places and people, how you can love them more fully and purely for who they are, rather than what they can give you. Notice what happens to the places that once scared you.

Chapter 3.2 – Family Culture

'Family culture' is still often invoked within organizations to convey a strong sense of unity and cohesiveness. We hear it in recruitment campaigns to attract talent or from eager to-be-employees who are excited to find belonging at their future workplace. While this can foster a strong sense of connectedness, this well-intended label anchors familial ties into a relationship that is inherently very different.

Take Rosie as an example, a bright-eyed fresh graduate, outgoing and ready to make her mark on the corporate world. Sporting an honours degree from the National University of Singapore, she was a top priority candidate for many organizations. After months of endless interviewing, she found herself narrowing her selection to three offers. The firms in consideration were equally reputable, with similar role responsibilities and career trajectories. There was one difference that stood out to her though: culture. She knew that if she was going to spend more than ten hours a day toiling away in an office, she would like to at least be working with people she bonded with.

So, when one of the companies described their work environment as 'family culture', a feeling of warm, encouragement, and support came over Rosie. She was drawn in by their stories of how they would do anything for each other and bought into their philosophy of protecting and supporting each other at all costs. Naturally, it was the one she chose.

The first week at work was great. There was an orientation for new joiners, where she immediately clicked with the people in her batch. They went to office on the same days, so they could see each other, have lunch together, and shared stories about their respective teams. The sense of camaraderie was strong. They bantered with each other on WhatsApp groups, and though they worked hard, they always had each other to share the stress with. The company also held exciting activities like beach parties, celebratory drinks, and team outings. Some teams were so close, they would go on weekend trips together!

Probation period passed and the work really started piling on. Luckily, Rosie's batchmates and teammates kept her motivated. Her manager frequently sent her emails in the late hours of the evening, which meant even when Rosie was out, she found herself constantly checking her phone. But she didn't mind it, because her manager was like an older sister to her. Moreover, Rosie knew her manager wasn't expecting a response right away, and that motivated her even more to be someone who was prompt and her manager could rely on. After all, a family is about sharing burden right?

A month passed.

Kenneth, her friend from the marketing team, went on a team weekend away the previous week, and apparently, it was ridiculously awesome. Rosie wasn't sure if her manager was aware, so she suggested the idea to her, saying it was something they could do as a team as well. But to her surprise, her manager, who was usually very open with her, reacted quite awkwardly, mumbling something about needing childcare. And, in the end, she said she will try.

Six months in.

It was a Monday morning. Rosie was staring at her computer in disbelief. Her manager was leaving. 'How could she do that to me?' played over and over in her head. Rosie was only six months in, and at the interview, her manager had promised to look after her and groom her into a fine professional. But now, she was leaving her behind. Rosie felt abandoned. Her manager was her work-sister, after all.

Later that morning, Rosie had a meeting with her manager. The moment she opened the door, her manager let out a big sigh. 'I'm so sorry,' she said. 'It was a really hard decision for me.'

What could be so hard? Rosie wondered. *We go through everything together.*

But as she sat there in silence, her manager continued. 'I have two young children. I had to leave work early to pick them up from school. Then, after cooking for them and putting them to bed, I would open my laptop again and work into the early hours of the morning. You did so much in responding to my emails late at night, and I feel guilty for leaving you behind. I feel equally bad for being unable to take the team out on weekend trips or join the celebrations. I know how important it was to the team.'

Rosie let out a gentle smile. 'It's okay,' she offered. 'You need to do what is right for you. I'll be okay.'

And with one long hug, she bid her farewell.

The departure of her manager was a big hit for Rosie, but having heard her side of the story, Rosie knew she was probably better off somewhere else. Having been thrown a bit off course, Rosie began to reorient herself and continued to work hard. She took on as much work as she could, progressed through the ranks, and was earmarked as a high potential. She took other new joiners under her wing, offering them the familial care and support she received as a newbie.

As she gained experienced, she was frequently selected to speak at events and appear on television to be the face of the business. She was the 'It' girl in the industry, and she proudly raved about her company whenever she got the chance. She came in early, finished late, and picked up the nickname 'Weekend Warrior', as she was frequently in the office on Saturdays and

Sundays. It took a toll on her health, but she kept going, because the company needed her.

Then, Covid-19 happened. It was June 2020; the virus was raging strong. Rosie was called into a meeting with HR and the Managing Director. After a robotic, rote-learned script was read to her, she was notified that her role was being made redundant, effective immediately. They said it was not due to her performance, so she shouldn't take it personally.

Not take it personally? she thought to herself. *But how?*

This was the home that had welcomed her in and told her she was family. Now, it is reduced to a soulless transaction which she shouldn't take personally?

Her mind flashed back to the months leading up to that day, where she had worked tirelessly to make sure the organization met its budget for the year. She had strained herself physically and emotionally, deprioritizing self-care in the pursuit of a vision that promised fruit for all.

And just like that, the familiar faces of those she had thought would protect her were now kicking her out. The previous day, they were family, and the following day, they would be strangers. Communication cut, laptop returned, and the few colleagues that reached out did so in a distant, awkward manner, usually starting with 'I heard the news . . .' or 'I hope you're okay . . .' almost as if she now had the responsibility to assure people that she was fine, so they could be free from their survivor's guilt. The feeling of 'I will fight for you through thick or thin,' dissipated into distance and silence, the bystander effect in full-swing. The struggle with the dissonance of supposed familial bonds with cold-hearted redundancy haunted her for months to come.

Eight years of belonging evaporated into what now feels like a distant memory.

The allure of belonging to a tight-knit workplace, can be warm and inviting. While the deep sense of emotional connection can be a powerful driving force for motivation and productivity, its misalignment with professional reality may mislead and cause devastating emotional impact when it ends. We may feel compelled to overextend ourselves, with a sense of attachment and responsibility akin to what we would offer to members of our family. For the manager that hired Rosie, the emotional weight of trying to conform to the familial-like expectations of a leader had ended up affecting her well-being and responsibilities as a mother.

When an organization operates like a family, the sense of belonging and shared purpose transcends formal policies, shaping behaviours and decisions in ways no rulebook ever could. It's a force that shapes identity, inspires commitment, and transforms a group of individuals into a unified community. The feeling of belonging to your colleagues, with your work-husbands, and work-wives makes even the toughest times doable and fun. They are your network of social support, buffering the impact of stress. They are your biggest cheerleaders, challenging and stretching you from a place of love and care.

The corporate family can be nourishing. It can ignite the spirit of unwavering loyalty and support of the company's mission. However, as wonderous and perfect this image is, it is often in stark contrast to the purpose and endeavours of the corporate world. We have a responsibility to ourselves and those around us to wake up to this reality. If we continue to use 'family culture' as a way of describing something that is driven by objectives and KPIs, we are wilfully misrepresenting an inherently transient relationship at the expense of employees.

For example, if we anchor familial ties to our corporate relationships, what does it mean to the sense of family as people resign, roles are made redundant, or new people are hired to replace them? As individuals, wake up to the words that you are fed. Our mind creates associations as a way of making sense of the world. So, whenever someone says 'family' to you, your mind, consciously or otherwise, draws on thoughts and emotions associated with family. Through repetition, those neural pathways are strengthened and those associations reinforced. Therefore, if your environment continues to misguide you, awaken to the fallacy, reclaim your perspective, and take over the steering wheel. Belonging is not unconscious followership; it is clarity in recognizing false appearances and refusing to let it define you.

In coaching leaders, one of the most common topics of conversation has revolved around the inner tug-of-war leaders felt between what the company wanted them to do and what felt true to them. For example, the introverted leader, who felt pressured to be the rah-rah extroverted leader because that was perceived to be the *right* way to lead. Or the leader, who was told they must manage people if they wanted to succeed, even though team management was never their definition of success. In coaching, conversations often included statements like, 'But I know I *should* . . .' to which I would ask, 'According to whom?' or 'What value are your honouring or betraying?'

This plays into Implicit Leadership Theory,[11] where we, individually and collectively, hold pre-existing beliefs about what makes an effective leader, then we drive ourselves and others to conform to it.

Shaped by organizational norms, personal experiences, and unspoken expectations, implicit leadership profiles are often based on reflections of the past, rather than what is required and needed in the present. For example, an organization that has typically had extraverted and charismatic leaders, who spend a lot of time outside work hours with their people, create implicit associations between those traits and leadership success. This misinterpretation may result in unconscious bias, where people who are naturally extroverted, charismatic, and have the capacity to constantly take their team out are continually rewarded, promoted, and accelerated in their careers. This forms a feedback loop which reinforces these ideals, resulting in people feeling the need to sacrifice their personal lives to meet these expectations if they want to progress.

While this perpetuates a cycle of sameness in leadership, compounded with a 'family culture', we not only mislead people into thinking their belonging is contingent on them fitting into a pre-existing model, but we also stifle innovation and creativity by valuing consensus over dissent and challenge. If we want to breed a culture of transparency, collective growth, and an understanding of corporate belonging that is closer to the truth, we need to rethink what it means to have a 'family culture'.

We can still enjoy the benefits of a tight-knit culture without calling it a family. If we can work with our eyes open to the true nature of our relationship with one another, we can still work hard and enjoy our time together—however, our commitments to each other would be built on the practical, transactional relationship that it really is, rather than grounded in familial ties. Perhaps, we can learn from Gen Z in adopting the nuanced word of 'situationship'—a label-less relationship. Although used in the context of romantic relationships, it captures the complexities of modern work relationships, where the traditional mutual commitments of loyalty no longer apply.

With frequent restructures becoming the norm, employment tenures shortening, matrix reporting lines, and talks of a future where job titles are abolished, a corporate-situationship is a much closer definition of what we now have with colleagues. With undefined roles, non-linear career paths, little certainty about when or how long we might work together, the corporate-situationship is fluid and adaptable. Unlike the notion of family culture, which implies unwavering loyalty and stability, a corporate-situationship embraces the reality of diverse, temporary, and portfolio professional engagements. It allows for collective performance without the burden of obligatory emotional ties.

Imagine how liberating this honesty in interactions can be. Instead of the pressure of harmony and familial belonging, we would feel more comfortable to express our differing views and ambitious, more inclined to lean into tension without the fear of damaging familial bonds, giving way to uncomfortable conversations that are ultimately the breeding ground for creative innovation.

In a recent workshop, the General Manager opened the session. 'Only take from this business the parts you like, don't swallow it whole,' he said. 'Learn from what we do well, and for the parts we don't, lead us towards what's better. I can't guarantee it will change the way you like, but I can guarantee you the permission to try. This is a company, not our home, and it's important we remember that. I am an employee too, just like you. So, do your best work while you're here, but remember to call your parents back, be with loved ones, and take time to do the things that light you up. I made that mistake early in my career, and that's why I only get to see my children two weekends a month.'

The participants were silent, but the silence wasn't empty—it was thick with reflection.

Imagine the greater courage we would have to be ourselves if we relinquished the need to play a defined role in the family narrative. We can still have mutual respect, understanding, and shared goals—we may even forge stronger bonds because we are coming together out of choice. The richness of professional relationships can flourish without the confines of a family label. Closeness and harmony are not necessarily definitions of a healthy workplace.

My role was made redundant in June 2024, after having been in the organization for a decade. 'Watch closely,' my mentor told me. 'This experience shows you, very quickly, the real nature of your relationships.' It felt like the end of a night of partying, when the music stops and all the lights come on, revealing the rawness of what was previously masked by neon glow and intoxication. It's one thing to hear it, and another to experience it. I must say, the scenes unfolded as though his words had already scripted reality.

Once the news was announced, everyone, almost instantaneously, moved into forming three clear groups. The first was made up of people with whom you knew your relationship wouldn't change—those who cared for you as a human being, beyond the business reasons that had initially brought you together. As expected, the second was the group that disappeared into the distance. We had come together as colleagues and separated as colleagues.

However, it was the third one that took me a while to process: the people who had proclaimed to be my family. They were colleagues I had confided in, drank with, stood up for—the ones who said they would always have my back. They acted much more like the second group of distant colleagues than anyone I would consider myself remotely close to. They stayed silent when I thought they would speak out; their farewells sounded like templated scripts used over a hundred times.

My mind went back to all the times I had believed, trusted, and defended them. The times I stayed silent to protect them when I should have spoken up. For a while, I even questioned my own sense of judgement. How could I have misread it so much? Who would have known that the words, 'We are like a family,' would have embedded into my subconscious, even though I knew it was not true logically?

Now, with some distance, I've realized how I had trapped myself in upholding this illusion of family. How, for the sake of 'bleeding blue'—which was a term we used to describe our loyalty to the business—I had betrayed my own values in support of family culture. I had convinced myself, and others, to accept certain behaviours because that's just who they were, instead of doing something about it.

I had traded in my trust for myself, for the trust of others; and for a while, it felt pretty good. The celebratory feedback you get when you fall in line misleads you to believe that you are walking in the right direction. We are rewarded with applause and promotions when we fall in line, and the shine of positive reinforcement can be so blinding that we mistake it for fulfilment.

When I think about the time I did my best work, it was after a time where I completely disconnected—from friends, family and colleagues. When I tuned out the endless advice I got from others and tuned into the voice of my heart. The people around us, although guided by noble intentions, are often echoing their own fears and aspirations.

During that time, I set out on a three-year-long journey to develop an in-house coaching function. In the beginning, there were more doubters than believers—including my own boss—but a knowing in me propelled me forward, stronger than any setback could ever push me back. My dream to give every leader the ability to access, at any time, a confidential session with an ICF Certified Coach, not because they were selected for a coaching programme or deemed worthy of investment. I called this team The Mindset Lab.

The unacknowledged need I saw in the workforce was not that leaders were not adequately 'developed', that is, taught the leadership skills required to succeed; but rather, they had no avenue to explore their innermost challenges and hesitations. Leadership can be lonely, and the higher you climb, the lonelier it gets. When you reflect on why you left your previous roles, it rarely boils down to a lack of capability. It's the unvoiced frustrations, the politics, suppressed emotions and relational mistrust that crusheds the spirit.

The Mindset Lab lets you break the rules, allows you to say unsayable things, confront truths that you feared would limit your career, allowing you the space to unpack them free from the clamour of everyone else's opinion, so you could finally hear your own.

Building The Mindset Lab was one of the most fulfilling things I've ever done. I could've never done it if I was still engrossed in the comfy fitout of my corporate family.

Family culture entices us to take well-trodden paths, yet the greatest adventures are those forged beyond them.

We are more phenomenal than competency frameworks, more capable than what shows up on personality tests, and more infinite than what a job title or organization can contain. The temporary enjoyment of being embraced by a 'family' silences the symphony of our own becoming.

Your heart knows a language that is uniquely yours. It is urging you to trust it as you chart a course that reflects your own dreams and aspirations.

REFLECTING

Feeling part of a 'family' work culture can be a beautiful thing, considering how much of our lives we spend on work. However, this corporate association with family can be wildly misleading, as the foundations of organizational culture are starkly different to that of family. This can easily lead to a pressure to conform, biased decision making, and a false expectation of mutual loyalty.

Ponder

- What does your workplace value and how do they compare with your own?
- Have you ever prioritized personal relationships in your company over professional responsibilities?
- Have you used or heard the description of corporate culture as 'family'? How does it resonate with you?
- What boundaries exist between your personal and professional life? When are they crossed?
- Have you ever stayed quiet and accepted a decision that was misaligned with your values?

Be Your Own Self Coach

When we honour our values, we feel full and energized. Conversely, when we betray our values, it leads to feelings of dissonance, avoidance, and regret. This disconnection with self can lead to burnout, decreased motivation, and mistrust in yourself. Pick up a pen and paper, envision you at your workplace. Connect with your energy, values, and beliefs. Now, draw a line that represents how aligned that environment is with you. The squigglier the line, the less aligned it is; the straighter, the more.

Take a look at that line. How does it feel to see in on paper? Examine the straighter parts: What do they represent? Now, do the same for squiggly parts: What do they represent?

What has come to your awareness that you did not notice before?

Beyonding

Below is a representation of you. Put into the head space, beliefs you hold about things that *must be*, or *should* remain the way they are. Include everything you can think of in your work and personal life. The expectations about what people *should* be for us, the things that *must* stay the same for things to be ok.

You can write each idea as a strand of hair, or you can represent it in colour shape and size. However it makes sense to you.

Notice the weight of these beliefs in your headspace. Notice the pressure we place on ourselves and others for things to remain a certain way. As you shed hair, what would you like to drop first?

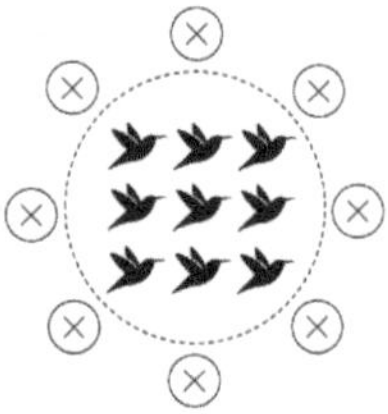

Chapter 4

DISSONANCE

Belonging has the power to distort decision making. There is a phrase in Chinese, **信息繭房** ('xìn xī jiǎn fáng'), which directly translates to 'information cocoon'. In English, we can think of this as echo chambers.

The phrase refers to the selective consumption of information we engage in when we belong to a group. We reinforce existing beliefs, preferences, and biases by creating an information cocoon around ourselves. Social media intensifies this through their algorithms, filtering our diverse perspectives and keeping us in an echo chamber.

This polarizing effect ends up leading us to strengthening our certainty of our beliefs, often closing our mind to conflicting views.

Chapter 4.1 – Certainty

Let's take a look at what happens when belonging meddles with our judgement.

Envisage this: You're at a social gathering, sipping your drink, when someone walks by wearing a t-shirt that smells like it has been marinating in a gym bag for a week. Your nose crinkles, and you feel the urge to vomit.

But wait!

Is that Steve from the American Club?

Suddenly, the stench morphs into a strangely nostalgic scent of camaraderie.

Welcome to the curious world of perception, where our ability to make accurate decisions can be totally thrown off by our level of connection. In some grossly fascinating studies, participants were asked to smell sweaty t-shirts bearing logos that would indicate whether its wearer was an in-group or out-group member.[12] They were to rate the t-shirt on a disgust Likert scale. For example, 'When I smelled this t-shirt, I was worried I would vomit,' or 'I'm indifferent to the smell of this person'.

Through self-reporting and measurement of behaviour, the studies concluded there to be an attenuation of disgust for in-group targets. This means that the participants felt less disgusted while smelling t-shirts of those whom they felt a sense of belonging with.

That's right!

The power of belonging made even the pungent, body-odour-drenched t-shirts smell acceptable.

How does this happen?

Turns out, when we feel a sense of belonging, it can significantly impair our judgement. Perception is the filter through which we see the world, and emotional connection softens even the harshest of appearances. And it's not just appearances—as the t-shirt study would demonstrate—group identities even influence our interpretation of basic sensory experiences.

Familiarity is likely to lead to more lenient evaluations of situations, as we unconsciously prioritize our emotional connection over the factual experience. Remember that time you walked into a room, and a familiar scent wafted through the air? Suddenly, a sense of warmth envelops you, or maybe, takes you right back to a memory you forgot existed. For me, this is Taiwanese stinky tofu, a scent I could bask in all day. For others, it would be considered as a form of modern day torture. This is called anchoring—the association of specific stimuli such as smell, sight, or sound, with a particular emotional state.

The person who appears to be a close friend or the rhythm of a song that reminds you of a melody played at your wedding are both likely to lead to a positive perception before you engage in any form of real evaluation. Smells are particularly powerful because you can reject certain stimuli by closing your eyes or blocking your ears. But not breathing becomes a little difficult!

This phenomenon raises important questions about the clarity of our judgement in the presence of belonging. While it's heartening to think that connections can make even unpleasant odours more palatable, it highlights how unreliable and easily influenced we are. We generally like to consider ourselves logical, fact-driven people; however, it's much easier to overlook flaws in the colleague we're closer to or take the wrongdoings of those we love lightly.

In the instance of the misjudged smelly t-shirts, the implications are minor. But what if there were more significant decisions, such as financial investments, access to resources, selecting the candidate to hire, or any choice that impacts lives of the people who depend on them? Belonging is the beautiful feeling that leads to misguided judgement, and we patch up the gaps in our reasoning by reverse manufacturing justifications that *appear* logical. Our emotional ties create blind spots, yet it feels nice to continually feed them as they reinforce our sense of belonging.

If you're shaking your head thinking, 'Nah . . . that's for people like so and so whom I know of, but that's definitely not me,' here is something for you.

Mentalist Derren Brown conducted a study that showed just how easily our views are swayed, even the ones we proclaim to be strongly held.[13] In this experiment, participants with right-wing and left-wing political beliefs were selectively shown images. Through measurement of their physical reactions, such as sweating and heart rate, it was found, as expected, that left-wingers—the progressives—were triggered by the weak and helpless, while the right-wingers—the conservatives—responded more to threats.

No surprises. The liberals are all about standing up for the weak, while the conservatives worry about protection against threats. They must have firm beliefs, be clear about what they stand for, and know which political party they support—right?

What if I told you that by simply creating a repulsive environment—like putting fake vomit on the ground and having them imagine the decomposition of a body after death—it was possible to get the liberals to answer questions on hot topics more conservatively?

Remember the smelly t-shirts in eliciting disgust? By inducing repulsion and fear of contamination with fake vomit, Brown was able to prime the liberals into feeling the need to protect themselves from threats, aligning with conservative views. Conversely, they were also able to get the conservatives to respond more liberally by asking them to envisage a state of invincibility, freeing them from feelings of threat.

We anchor convictions with unwavering certainty, yet they are more like shifting sand in the wind. Each time the direction of the wind changes, or the humidity increases in the air, our seemingly steadfast views shift: just like a rock by the shore, though sitting in apparent stillness, is endlessly being shaped and reshaped by its environment—smoothed by water, cracked by the sun's heat, weathered down by storms. In our quest for certainty, we should be reminded that even our strongest beliefs are porous and fragile.

We've all heard of the two-faced leader: someone who champions well-being, people-centricity, creativity, and innovation when things are good. However, when pressure hits, they change their tune faster than superman changes his clothes. The values they once spoke of now feel redundant, and if ever questioned, a standard 'It was a necessary business decision,' answer is given. Soon, meetings with them shift from 'Ask me anything,' to focusing solely on financial metrics and performance targets. Employees who were motivated by what the leader stood for begin to feel disillusioned, questioning whether they ever meant anything they said before. The atmosphere shifts from one of trust and collaboration to one of competition and fear.

As for the leader, they deny they are straying from their commitment. They point to forces above or around them to justify their difference in behaviour, reinforcing that they are still the same person. To maintain this certainty, they might even create a mental separation between their work-self and the *real* one to compartmentalize their identity. All this, so they can make choices that are misaligned with what they had once said without admitting that they have changed or regressed.

They convince themselves that they were necessary decisions for the greater good and merely doing what was best for the company. This is a common occurrence captured in fallback theory,[14] where under stress, uncertainty, or fear, people tend to revert to older, less evolved patterns of behaviour. These include ways of thinking, responding, or acting that feel familiar and safe, even if it no longer serves their highest intentions or best interests.

This fallback is a form of regression, where people abandon more advanced coping mechanisms or leadership approaches and return to rudimentary stages of development. Leaders who embraced openness and transparency may revert to authoritarian decision-making, employees who were proactive and adaptable may retreat into compliance and silence, and the sharing of ideas revert to siloed, protectionist ways of working. When we feel safe, we feel brave and expand vertically, even proudly advocating our belonging to these higher ways of being.

Yet, at any moment, we can be triggered to shrink back into smaller versions of ourselves. The challenge here is not about how do we stop fallback from happening, but rather, how do we accept fallback as a part of our lives. We must own up to the fact that *that* two-faced leader is not just 'someone else'; we have been that person too.

We just don't like to admit it, because acknowledging it can feel like failure or weakness. It goes against the certainty of 'knowing' who we are. We are only supposed to go from strength to strength, and growth is defined by a constant uphill trajectory. That's what the world teaches us.

Our need to feel like we are something stable causes us to categorize and label ourselves with closed narratives. Our desire to define ourselves is natural, but the self we seek has always been fluid, never solid. Our perceptions are bias and easily influenced; our identities ever changing. We are much more a jumbled collection of quirks and contradictions than the perfectly curated logical humans we like to think we are.

We refuse to accept that we move like puppets on strings, finding whatever reasons we can to justify the gross inaccuracies in our decision making. We claim to stand firm on our beliefs, living in an illusion of certainty when we are every colour of the rainbow. Instead of embracing the fluidity of our being, we cling to well-rehearsed stories about who we are.

The illusion of certainty can feel like a sigh of relief when placed next to messiness. But it is in this messiness that we begin our work of creative recovery, bringing back the person we left behind: ourselves.

Think back to the last time you introduced yourself to a stranger, the words you said, the titles you mentioned. Now, imagine you are in a sea of Lego, splattered with every colour and shape you can think of. Build a representation of yourself with it. What colours and shapes would you pick? How would they come together? Now, compare what you have built to the standard introduction you offer to strangers. That's the difference.

We draw defined lines around our identity, expending all our energy in conforming with what those titles require. And if our identity ever feels threatened, we prioritize security over exploration. The more we are entrenched in the roles we *must* play, and the beliefs we *must* uphold, the deeper divide we create between our inner truth and the mask we wear.

If instead, we welcome the ambiguous nature of ourselves, we switch our limited view for infinite possibility. We release energy from the exhausting need to defend our sense of belonging to rigid labels, freeing up space for us to channel it into imagination and creativity. The world opens up, and so do we.

To help you along, befriend an outlier. Outliers challenge the frameworks we take for granted, reminding us how fragile our certainties and assumptions are. When we feel the onset of comfort-like belonging, actively seek dissenting voices. The active engagement in discourse forces us to question the constructs we cling to. The discomfort of hearing opposing views is the growing pain as our world expands. Feel it, embrace it, and sit with it as it brings you beyond your previous reality. The counterintuitive nature of moving toward tension is exactly what needs to happen if we want to reverse the narrowing of our world.

Think of that person in your family or organization who stands out like a sore thumb. They speak up, go against the grain, and are the 'difficult' one—the one who always has an opinion about everything. Over time, their voice gets drowned out, their opinions pushed aside, and they are labelled as 'not a team player'.

I worked with a CFO who was hired for their experience, yet ignored every time they tried to use it. While bringing them onboard, the company had told them they wanted a right-hand person to the CEO, who would push boundaries and take the business to greater heights. But in reality, they just wanted an operational CFO who would obediently nod in agreement.

Outliers are typically rejected in scientific studies, mislabelled as toxic in organizations, and outcasted by communities. This process of expulsion and ostracization is why we continue to unknowingly confine ourselves in smaller and smaller boxes.

Our judgement against what does not belong, turns into fear and protection. We repel them with disgust and sever ties to protect our own belonging in the group. We double-down on our beliefs and we proudly call it 'standing firm'. We turn and nod to our neighbours to triple check we are indeed doing things 'right'—and all this while, there is an outlier just beyond your doorstep, ready to tip over your table of certainties, just to show you it was too small to hold you anyway.

Sometimes, they smile; at times, they shout in frustration. Other times, that outlier is another person; but, at times, our own inner voice. Sometimes, we grow so unconscious that our intuition fights to break us free. The tension we feel might not be because of other people, but a war within ourselves. When we get so used to letting the world tell us what to do, our voice of intuition gets quieter and quieter. It never disappears, though. It's always there, just beyond the worldly anchors we grow attached to.

At times, it pipes up in the form of sudden clarity; other times, it signals to you through physical symptoms. It knows that you were destined for more, and it never gives up on you. Whenever it feels like you might hear it, it calls out to you, and if you choose to listen, it gets louder. It invites you to see more, be more, and uncover your messy, weird, and wonderful self.

This freedom, which need not be defined by a group or label, is the breeding ground of wisdom. This discovery is where we allow what was previously unseen to emerge from its hiding place.

We were never lost in the messiness; there is magic in it, and we always knew where to go. We just got confused when we let the voice of the collective override the voice of our truth.

For all the effort we spend on trying to *find* who we are, if we learn to release and let go, we will remember.

REFLECTING

A simple change in environment can shift even the strongest opinions we claim to hold, and at any moment, we are susceptible to falling back into outdated, regressed versions of ourselves. Our proud parade of belonging to a fixed sense of self with unwavering beliefs is an illusion that hinders us from uncovering the transformative magic of messiness.

Ponder

- What truths about yourself are you avoiding?
- What aspects of your identity do you cling to that may be limiting?
- When have you rejected an outlier, even though you agreed with where they were coming from?
- Who is an outlier you'd like to reach out to?
- When do you fallback?

Be Your Own Self Coach

Confronting the illusion of certainty can be scary, and your willingness to face the uncomfortable is a testament to your courage. Venturing into the places that scare us is the leap of faith we take to explore the infinite beyond. This is a visualization that will help you embrace your fallback patterns and how they manifest in your life.

Picture yourself standing at the beginning of a tranquil forest as you start your hike up a mountain. Surrounding you are towering trees, vibrant forests and gentle rustling leaves. This forest represents your journey of maturity and growth. As you start climbing, feel the sense of accomplishment you gain as you make your way upwards, higher and higher. You see a clearing in the distant bathed in sunlight, and as you climb, the brighter and warmer the sun feels.

You take a deep breath and take a big step up into the sunlight when you suddenly feel your foot slip on the surface beneath you. As you gasp and feel your whole body tighten, you feel yourself stumble backwards into the shadows. Just like that, you fell back into a much earlier time and place, representing a part of you that you surpassed long ago, and now you're right back there.

What was it that you slipped on? What do you see in this place now that you didn't when you were last here? Take a deep breath and sink in to the learns of this moment, knowing that there is no failure, only feedback. Embrace it, thank it. What is present for us to understand? What is here for you to learn?

Chapter 4.2 – Cognitive Dissonance

In the early-1950s, a group of followers gathered around the leadership of Dorothy Martin, also known as Mrs. Keech.[15] She was a passionate leader who believed she had a special connection with aliens. The group of believers she brought together were called the Seekers.

Mrs Keech claimed to receive instructions from the 'Guardians', a group of supposed extraterrestrial beings that she communicated with. At times, they would 'order' her to do simple tasks, such as be at certain places at certain times. Other times, she would be given predictions of specific future events. The Seekers believed with unwavering conviction that a great flood would sweep through earth on 21 December 1954, sparing only those who believed in Mrs. Keech's message. Those who were 'ready', and were believers, would be rescued by aliens. For the Seekers, this prophecy was not just a prediction; it was a lifeline, a promise of salvation in a chaotic world.

Among them was Leon Festinger, a social psychologist who infiltrated the group, and was studying them discreetly. Intrigued by the power of group dynamics, he participated in their rituals and discussions, blending into their tightly knit community with a sense of belonging made up of fervent spirituality, emotional support, identity, and purpose. They shared stories of personal experiences, dreams, and fears. They prayed, meditated, and received communication from the Guardians.

The communal atmosphere was electric. Each member found solace in knowing they were part of a mission that transcended their individual lives. This collective identity offered not only comfort, but a framework through which they understood their place in the world. Festinger felt the captivating nature of Mrs. Keech each time she spoke, and watched their commitment intensify as they gathered to pray and chant as the date approached. Their belief was air-tight, drowning out any scepticism. The Seekers provided a sanctuary from a world that often felt indifferent or hostile.

Then, the day came.

The clock ticked towards midnight, and the Seekers waited, hearts racing with expectation. As the hours passed and the apocalypse did not occur, a heavy silence descended. The flood never came. Reality, stark and undeniable, shattered their carefully constructed beliefs. Confusion flickered in the eyes of some, while others wore expressions of shock.

However, unlike the 'wake up' we would expect from someone whose beliefs have just been proven wrong, a strange transformation began to take shape in the group.

Instead of abandoning their beliefs, the Seekers doubled-down in a profound act of psychological contortion, bending facts until they no longer threatened their faith. We call this 'cognitive dissonance'. Cognitive dissonance is the discomfort we feel when we hold conflicting beliefs simultaneously. For the Seekers, it was their belief in the apocalypse alongside the uncomfortable truth of their failed prediction. The theory of cognitive dissonance lay out that people work to alleviate the discomfort by creating narratives that rationalizes the situation, instead of confronting the truth.

The Seekers concluded that their unwavering faith had somehow intervened, altering the course of destiny hence why the flood never came. By doing so, they resolved the discomfort of cognitive dissonance through denial, and protected their self-concept.

Festinger saw how they not only survived the disconfirmation of the prophecy, but clung even tighter to their convictions. Failure was, therefore, not a catalyst for rethinking, but evidence of their faith's power.

In the case of the Seekers, the members' need for belonging intensified their response. The group's bonds created an emotional blindfold against the harsh truths outside their bubble, and to relinquish those would mean to tear down the foundations of their belonging to each other.

As the weeks went by, the Seekers continued to hold meetings, not in despair, but with renewed vigour. Each gathering became an opportunity to dissect their experiences, reinforcing their collective identity. Festinger observed that the cognitive dissonance they experienced was not just a personal struggle. Instead, it became a shared journey, a testament to their loyalty to one another, and to the vision that had initially brought them together.

The Seekers is as key example of how belonging can create a protective cocoon, shielding individuals from the contradicting realities of the outside world—all the while silencing our inner voice of reason.

Festinger's study of the Seekers became a compelling exploration of group dynamics. Not only do we willingly come together to belong to one another, we conform, establish joint beliefs, then we close ourselves off to information that challenges the validity of those beliefs. The greater the control and domination, the more likely that incongruent evidence is reinterpreted to allow continuation of belonging. To dismantle a belief system would be too traumatic to confront, so, instead, we seek refuge in group thinking during times of contradiction, alleviating us from the discomfort of dissonance.

Many other similar studies on religious prophecies show surprising commonalties.[16] Eleven out of thirteen groups were found to survive a failure of prophecy, although their reasons for survival and patterns of response were different.

As outsiders, it is easy to look into cult behaviour and judge those who become ensnared in such groups. We might think, 'That's so stupid! How could they believe such things?'

Yet, we are more susceptible than we like to believe.

The Seekers drew people in not merely because of its prophecy, but because it was a place where members felt safe from ridicule. Our need to feel seen and heard can lead us to gravitate towards embracing even the most tenuous beliefs. We can all probably think of someone who is caught up in a community that proselytizes questionable ideologies.

However, instead of engaging in healthy discourse to verify the validity of their beliefs, they switch off their ears and close their hearts for their belonging to the group is more important than reason.

Cults or fundamentalist groups, often draw people in during times of struggle or vulnerability. People who seek a higher power for guidance, certainty, and salvation. This is particularly attractive when we are conditioned to believe that our world is cold and alienating.[17] Endlessly drowned by distressing news headlines, we are conditioned to focus on all that's wrong in the world.

There will be forces that entice us into tight-knit group dynamics, but the intensity with which we allow it to consume us is in our control. Spotting red flags—clear lines between 'us' and 'them', 'good' and 'bad', and limiting of contact with those outside the group—can be signals to actively go beyond your place of belonging to sense check your ideologies. Detachment is sometimes the necessary discomfort to keep yourself awake in a system that wants you to stay asleep.

These environments are not unique to cults and religions. Take, for example, the work environment, where your ability to climb is often linked with your willingness to align with dominant views. It fosters a sense of camaraderie and belonging, and often has practical implications too—that is, if you fit in, the value of your work is given more attention and you are offered more resources.

For some, fitting in feels natural; for others, it may be about fitting in to survive. The company culture can be alluring: the swag and perks, cool colleagues, and a steady schedule of social events. Our eagerness to be part of a team gets put to the test once we start noticing behaviours and decisions that conflict with our personal values. Perhaps, it is the value of fairness, or that of honesty and integrity. The witnessing of questionable practices to get numbers across the line, or being asked to participate in grey-area practices.

Take yourself back to a time when that happened: What did you do? How did it feel?

If the answer in your heart is that you stayed quiet and went along with it, what did that do to you? How did sitting with that dissonance impact your connection with yourself?

It's not an uncommon story, staying in line instead of standing out, convincing ourselves that 'Everyone else does it,' to justify our participation. But what happens to us when we do it over and over? What does the separation of 'work me' and 'real me' do to our psyche?

Or, perhaps, it has become so second nature that you don't even notice it. Cognitive dissonance is like a quiet thief—stealing from us bit by bit, until the person staring back in the mirror is a stranger. Then we wonder why we feel like we have lost ourselves.

Family dynamics can also serve a hefty dose of cognitive dissonance. The pressure to be performative in meeting familial expectations, can create deep internal conflict. The desire for acceptance and validation often leads to the suppression of our true aspirations. We manage this dissonance by convincing ourselves of the practical considerations like financial security or family responsibility, reciting seemingly logical rationales for why we do what we do, while unfulfillment lingers.

I worked with a woman once, Annie, who faced extreme pressure from her family to stop working when she became a mother. 'I wouldn't describe myself as a super go-getter career woman, but working is important to me,' she said. 'It's my way of feeling relevant in this world.' However, when she returned to work after maternity leave, every little mishap that happened at home was indirectly attributed to her. 'I heard that your friend Lisa just stays home now with her son,' Annie's mom would say to her. 'It's so nice that Toby [Lisa's son] can come home to his mom every day.' Small jabs to the side while never confronting her directly. 'The kids have to catch the school bus home?' her mother-in-law would ask. 'Hmm . . . poor things.'

No matter how much she shared with them what it meant to her that she could still contribute to the working world, there was little interest in hearing her out. Then one day, she gave in. She quit her job and became a full-time housewife. She stayed home, while her husband worked. Her friends comprised of parents from school and her routine revolved around school, cooking, and cleaning—rinse and repeat. 'I stopped introducing myself by my first name,' she told me half-jokingly. 'I'm now Chris' or Katie's mom.' She laughed, but not the laugh I remembered from before; it was as if some of the lustre in her had faded.

What surprised me the most was when I met her again, several years later. 'The kids are older now,' I said. 'How about picking back up where you left off? I know someone that would be interested in speaking to you.'

'Oh no, no, no,' she replied. 'The kids need me.' She proceeded to tell me how she is glad she has the financial stability, so she could be a good mother to her children. How she was probably not cut out for a career, anyway. Speaking to her felt strange and eerie, as if her mother was speaking through her but I could still sense Annie trapped inside. I may be wrong, she may have changed her tune and found light on the other side, but something didn't feel quite right.

In some instances, doing the 'right' thing may even feel soul destroying, but abandoning the path would come with too much guilt.

The desire to meet family expectations can be overwhelming, especially when they are the place that many would say we belong, or we *should* belong. The difficult tug-of-war between wanting to please the people who loved, raised and cared for us, and living a life true to ourself is a common dilemma—especially when paving our own path can be construed as selfishness.

While no one is guaranteed to walk our life with us but ourselves, family ties tend to outlast those of others that come and go. Regardless, many of us reach a point in our lives where our efforts to resolve dissonance is no longer able to contain our overflowing inner struggle.

Let's peer into the build-up.

Long before we reach our breaking point, our bodies have already signalled to us to wake up. Its manifestation as physical ailments—anxiety, headaches, stomach aches—are often overlooked. Instead of pausing and asking ourselves, 'What might my body be trying to tell me?', we drown it with medication and logical justifications. 'I must have pulled something at the gym.' Or 'Maybe it was from sitting too long or a change in the weather.' Of course there is the possibility that it is a pure physical injury, however, rarely do we consider its link to emotional burden or subconscious tension. Our treating of symptoms silences our body's communication with us as we continue toiling through unfulfilling, unaligned lives.

The long-term pull between conflicting realities can lead to much greater issues than temporary discomfort.

Consider the analogy of baking a cake.

Anyone who has baked before would be familiar with the feeling of watching your cake rise in the oven, and just as you are about to sing your self-praise song, for some reason unknown to you, it suddenly flops. However, because there is no time to bake another cake, we convince ourselves that it will be fine, we can hide it under layers of icing! And so we do, lathering on layers of fondant and decoration.

To the outsider, the cake is perfect. However, we know it hides an unstable core. This is representative of our cognitive dissonance: Each time we push aside the calling of our knowingness, we add another layer of icing, trying to maintain the cake's appealing look, while covering the cracks forming underneath. On the outside, we are polished and perfect. However, beneath is a cake that risks collapsing, especially as the weight of the fondant builds.

Representative of our adaptative mechanisms, the more layers we continue to lather on, the further we get from our core. We might be aware of what is happening, but it's way easier to keep adding on layers than to face what we might find inside. After a while, resolving dissonance becomes so habitual that we grow oblivious to our own behaviour. We grow numb to the signals of our body, and we buy into the illusion of the beautiful exterior, convincing ourselves that that's who we really are.

The interesting thing with life is that it someway, somehow, finds its way to bring us the truth. Such as through the infamous mid-life-crisis, where we suddenly throw our whole life into question, and wonder if we missed the exit to our own dreams.

The popularized quarter-life-crisis shows how, even in the early stages of our career, we may have already walked a path that is incongruent with our true interests. Burnout, depression, and resentment can all be manifestations of festering cognitive dissonance. Left unaddressed and unprocessed, it will bleed into our relationships, creating strain or blame, leading to more distance, guilt or withdrawal from those we love.

We must raise our awareness of what is happening within us. If we can lean into the tension, acknowledge cognitive dissonance, and practice speaking our truth, we have the chance to free ourselves from the potential carnage of continually suppressed emotions. If we choose the path of least resistance, brush aside our own voice for the sake of acceptance and momentary peace, the burden we pile on has the power to one day break us. And when that day comes, the journey home to yourself will be a long and treacherous one.

Let's, instead, picture an alternative.

We can make the difficult, yet empowering choice, to awaken. We do this by bravely bracing ourselves for disapproval, while actively seeking dissenting views, challenging the stories of the group to spark our inner truth. The tighter our circle of belonging, the easier it is for us to lose sight of our inner truth. When you seek out outliers, you need not agree with the new perspective you're given, but simply listen with an open mind while asking yourself: 'Is there a part of me that also challenges my current reality?' Understanding the logic of the 'enemy', the 'other side' the rebellious outlier, is the key to your expansion, and you have every power to obtain it.

Remember that curious kid who always asked, 'Why?' That 98 per cent potential for creative genius—they are still a part of you. Invite them out for a play date.

When was the last time you stopped, closed your eyes, and felt what is going on inside you? Our mind can play tricks on us but our body speaks the truth. We use our mind to alleviate dissonance, but our bodies are not so easily fooled. Next time, when something feels a little off, instead of ramping up your mind to override the intelligence of your body, connect with it and ask it: What are you trying to tell me?

The closer we are to an experience, the less we see. The stronger the attachment, the more need there is to tune into how it's influencing you. This is not about denying yourself the benefits of belonging, but rather, allowing yourself a regular alignment check, so you can be both the subjective experiencer and objective observer of your reality.

REFLECTING

Cognitive dissonance is the mental discomfort we feel when we hold contradicting beliefs.

For example, when we are part of a group, our sense of identity becomes entwined with shared belief, values, and goals. While this belonging fuels our emotional needs and offers comfort, when faced with information that contradicts the group's beliefs, we are likely to change the story in our minds to align the new evidence to our belief, rather than challenge the group. This is the tension between what we know and what we want to believe, and people will often choose to rationalize, ignore, or deny conflicting evidence to maintain their place in the group.

While the example of the cult was used, this can arise in any environment where there is a strong sense of belonging and identity. If we want to awaken to this, it requires creating space for the emergence of our inner truth, and fostering critical thinking. This allows for a belonging that enriches rather than restricts, supporting personal authenticity while enjoying community ties.

Ponder

- What beliefs or values do I hold that feel misaligned with my current environment?
- When I experience discomfort or tension around a belief, how do I respond?
- Who am I afraid of disappointing or alienating if I embrace my own truth over the group's belief? How realistic are these fears?

Be Your Own Self Coach

Be brave and experience the tension for a moment. Connect with where it shows up, and simply observe it. There is nothing you need to do or fix—all there is to do, is to fully acknowledge your inner conflict, without needing to justify or change anything. As you observe, ask yourself: What is the cost of ignoring or justifying this discomfort? How does it impact my sense of authenticity, well-being, and relationships with others?

If a friend were in your shoes, what advice would you offer them? What is that one small action you could take to align your actions more closely with your values, even if it means stepping slightly outside the group's expectations?

Beyonding

Draw the tree below twice in the boxes provided. First, draw it with your dominant hand. Then, repeat the drawing, but this time, with your non-dominant hand.

Enjoy the experience, laugh at your own awkwardness.

Left	Right

On the drawing with your dominant hand, write words you *want* to be associated with: confident, capable, logical, reasonable—for instance. On the drawing by your non-dominant hand, write words that spontaneously arise for you as you look at this picture: messy, silly, weak—to name a few.

These trees *combined* represent your tree of life. While we like to associate ourselves with a certain image, we must remember that the reverse also exists. The tighter we cling to the righteousness of our ideologies, the more we resist the messy, illogical, contradictory parts of ourselves. If we close ourselves off to only acknowledging the parts we like, then we deny ourselves the ability to see and love ourselves wholly. We are all uncertain, ever-changing, evolving, and constantly contradicting ourselves. If we can accept this, then we also become more curious in hearing out information or beliefs that challenge our worldview.

Chapter 5

HAPPINESS

Ahh, the elusive happiness!

The harder we search for it, the more difficult it is to find. We are socialized into believing that happiness is to be obtained—an endeavour outside ourselves that stems from money and consumption. The harder we work, the more we consume, we live under the false pretence that one day, when we've consumed enough, we will be happy.

We get a housing mortgage, a car, then another one, and pile on more responsibilities to keep ourselves trapped—running faster and faster as our need for money increases.

Happiness is the moving target that we never seem to reach. What if, instead, we scrapped the formula and tried something new? What if we redirect our energy expenditure from money and consumption towards connecting with our sense of self?

How does belonging contribute to this?

Chapter 5.1 – The Search for Happiness

Happiness—the most paradoxical pursuit in modern life.

On one hand, happiness is celebrated as the ultimate life goal: a marker of fulfilment and purpose. On the other hand, it is rarely regarded as a measure of success in the world, where productivity, performance, and profits are prioritized.

Happiness in the workplace, at best, may be attributed to engagement scores in an annual HR survey. In our professional lives, it is often sidelined as something to be found outside of work hours, the elusive 'work-life balance', where work is widely accepted as the place you earn a living from, and happiness is the extra stuff you can aim for in your free time.

The irony lies in how we treat happiness as both essential and dispensable. Essential in our personal lives, yet dispensable in the workplace. 'A job is called a job for a reason,' I was once told. 'If its aim was to make us happy, then we would call it play.' Yet, we seem to pursue some form of happiness through career achievements, hoping that promotions or pay rises will bring us closer to it. We feel a buzz when we close in on a target. Then, we plummet to normalcy shortly after we achieve it.

The high of the dopamine hit traps us in a cycle of wanting *more*. The psychological concept of hedonic adaptation shows us that the joy we seek never lasts long. Our brains adapt quickly to the new high, and before we know it, we're asking, 'What's next?'

For example, winning the lottery or buying a new pair of shoes can offer happiness. However, a few days or weeks later, the residual happiness is almost indiscernible.

These spikes can also come from the removal of a stimulus: for example, work.

When we feel stressed or burnt out, we opt for time off or a holiday. After gaining temporary relief, we feel happy. However, the moment we are back at work, it doesn't take long for us to be right back where we started. We make it bearable by planning another holiday in the future, giving ourselves something else to work towards. Each time these external rewards come up short, we are left wondering whether enduring happiness exists at all, or whether it is a concept that belongs on a pedestal—a way of life to strive for but we never directly experience.

In 2018, my whole world narrowed to one obsession. How can I feel happiness again? I was struggling with even the simplest everyday tasks. I carried a dark cloud with me wherever I went. Waking up in the morning was painful; my head still cloudy from the bottle of wine I drank each night to put myself to sleep. It was as if something completely severed my emotions from me, and I had lost the capacity to feel. All the things I once found funny felt grey and emotionless; I didn't feel happy or sad—or anything at all, really. I was living in a vacuum, void of all connection with society, and myself. Everything felt meaningless.

At work, I remember being asked to be involved in applying for an award for the company. My immediate thought was, 'This is a PR stunt. I bet we rigged the results.' That lens of absolute pessimism painted my whole world, and the drag of being alive consumed me. I remember thinking: *If there was a button I could press to be done with this lifetime and move onto the next, I'd do it.*

Suicide was a daily thought, and alcohol was my only companion. It was my runaway car in my race away from myself.

I had just gone through a breakup, my grandfather wasn't well, and I felt stagnant at my job. This concoction of seemingly manageable events, if considered independently, crept up on me one by one as I noticed myself spiral downhill.

My worried mom and grandmother came to visit me. I remember sitting at my dining table, while my mom urged me to return to Sydney and seek help. I could see the pain in her eyes as she desperately tried to connect with me; however, all I remember was feeling void of all emotions as I looked at her.

One morning, at work, a colleague approached me. 'Do you think you might be depressed, Judy?' he asked.

It was the first time I had heard someone use the word 'depressed' to describe me. Usually, I'm the bubbly sunshine that lights up the room. I was a little taken aback, but in hindsight, it made perfect sense. I was numb to life. Even though I was still a part of the world, I felt completely separated from everyone in it.

Then, one day, a subordinate approached me. 'Boss, are you okay? You haven't felt quite right for a while.'

That was the last straw.

For the first time in a while, I felt something—anger. I felt so angry and disappointed in myself. While I was fine with this sense of drowning at a personal level, I felt it was irresponsible and selfish of me to pull down my team with me.

That same day, I resigned from my job.

However, after several conversations with my manager, we decided I would go on a sabbatical instead. Back then, this concept was uncommon, and it was genuinely kind of them to make that case for me. 'That way,' they said, 'you'll still be able to keep your insurance and benefits. And with so much mess in your life, maybe work can be your pillar of support.'

The leaders involved in that decision were the best ones I've met in my life.

With that, I set off in search for happiness. I packed my bags and made my way to Thailand. My friend had recommended checking out a meditation centre. He had just returned from a retreat, and I remember the glow and warmth of his aura when he met me.

Although I was already in the habit of drinking a bottle of wine each night, I was clear that I had two choices: I could continue to drink, party, and keep numbing myself from this experience; or I could sit with the discomfort of my own being.

Somehow, I knew that the answer was within me. However, a part of me felt stupid enough to trust that voice because up until then, I was rewarded for shunning feelings and prioritizing *thinking* over *feeling*.

I was known as the 'hardcore', 'black and red Judy', as my colleague described: bitchy, unfriendly, though excellent at what I did. I would say things like, 'Trust your head; your heart is a fool,' or 'Hey, look at the floor. I think you dropped your brain. Next time, try picking it up and putting it in your head before you talk to me.'

A repeated feedback I received was that I am all head and no heart—that I lacked empathy. Though, a part of me kind of liked that label. I saw it as a representation of toughness, and I was rewarded for it. I was the funny mean girl—funny only if you weren't on the other side of my ridicule. When I look back now, I don't even recognize myself. In fact, when I describe that old version of me to people who didn't know me back then, they shake their heads in disbelief!

So, at that time, the idea of intuition was foreign and fluffy to me. It felt like a gentle, elusive fabrication of my imagination, rather than anything concrete to be relied upon. But I guess, karma had been keeping score of my terrible behaviour, and the universe had decided it was time to put me to work, the *real* work—and so I did.

I lived by myself, learnt about meditation, and practiced it four to six hours a day. I ate by myself, living a life of isolation.

For the first month, I woke up frustrated each day over not having progressed. I kept thinking, 'Why the hell do I still feel like this?', 'Why am I still following this stupid voice inside me? This is not working.' It felt as if I was stuck inside a storm with no sign of an exit.

Meditation was no joke. To this day, I still feel like a noob, even though I've maintained a daily practice since. In the process though, I came to understand a thing or two about the mind.

People tend to be more familiar with concentration meditation over contemplative one: for example, clearing your mind and concentrating on your breath. This practice involves keeping your mind anchored on a single object. While its seemingly simple, it was incredibly difficult for me.

The discovery of contemplative meditation helped me a lot. Unlike concentration meditation, contemplative meditation is where you are, as the name suggests, actively using your mind to 'contemplate'. Usually, it is exploring an idea or a concept, which can feel active, laborious, and completely opposite to peace and serenity. The meditation centre gave me a practice to repeat for weeks. It involved dividing my lifeline into decades: zero to ten, ten to twenty, twenty to thirty, and so on.

Later, I was told to sink into each decade and allow memories within that timeframe to surface. Each time a memory emerged, I would acknowledge it, move it into a furnace in front of my mind's eye—sending it into the flames and letting it go. It was about allowing me to experience my life again, but this time, from the perspective of a non-attached observer. The motion of moving it into the furnace was to reinforce non-attachment, separating the emotional weight I carried.

To my surprise, I was instructed to do this with all memories, not just the negative ones. This recollection felt endless: good, bad, forgotten memories—some felt so foreign that I wondered if they were even mine. I tensed up each time an uncomfortable memory surfaced, and felt a soreness of longing as I watched beautiful memories float into the furnace. It was like Marie Kondo had entered my mind, going on a rampage to throw away my mental belongings. I spent hours each day clearing out my mental house—just that I didn't get to keep the things that brought me joy; everything had to go!

While each day felt like an intense mental workout, every time I finished the exercise, my mind felt lighter. Physically, it felt like a room had opened in my head—although, by the next morning, it would start to clutter again.

The clarity I felt after each intensive meditation kept me going: like that big sigh of relief, knowing you did a good job after an hour at bootcamp. Perhaps it was the intensity of proactive mind activity that felt satisfying, or maybe it was the nudge of my intuition that kept me going.

Then, things began to change.

I was faced with some confronting realizations.

I had built a world around me based on blame, where I was the righteous, misunderstood victim, and the wrongdoers should have done better. It repeated in all areas of life: work, family, romantic relationships. I was a perennial victim of this world—powerless and alone. No one was ever going to understand me. My narrative was written from a place of pain, and my ego was doing all that it could to fill the void. I was closing in on myself, and my greatest fear was to open up, as that place of openness would be like standing unarmed in a war zone; I wasn't sure if I could survive another hit. Each time I purged and sent memories into the furnace, it was like letting go of a paragraph from my million-page story. However, slowly as the paragraphs fell away, the grasping intensity I once felt began to ease.

At some point, my need to have a firm 'identity' eased too—not from a sense of loss, but a realization of the looseness of identities. What is an identity anyway, if not a list of labels given to us or we give ourselves? We accumulate them like scout badges to meet others' expectations or in seek of their validation. But, at the end of the day, badges are just badges.

So, does it even matter?

Why are we consumed with collecting badges on a vest, when who we really are is what existed before we put them on? The notion of a clear-cut identity suddenly seemed nonsensical, because badges change: We add some, remove some. So, why do we let them define us?

As I moved down that path of inquiry, I began experiencing what I've heard people call 'Life'—the river of consciousness that makes up our being.

Not 'life' in the clinical sense, referring to the events of our passing days. But Life, with a capital L, that describes the aliveness that is ever-present, an energy that reverberates with a wholeness that I find difficult to put to words. Life does not shift on a good or bad day, nor does it discriminate between positive or negative. Take, for example, a strong emotion—such as anger—if we tune into it, connect to it, and feel it, it is full of Life.

Imagine this: The next time someone displays anger, flipping out in front of you. Instead of getting caught in their whirlwind by clinging onto the words they say, which will only but fuel your own anger, connect with their Life. Move beyond the words and big swinging arm movements, and instead, sense the sameness of their Life with yours. Notice how this awareness of connection dissipates feelings of separation. Compassion for our shared Life shifts us from surface-level categorizations to a profound sense of oneness.

As this awareness dawned upon me, fleeting aspects of 'life', with a lower case 'l', began to fade in importance: material possessions, job titles, status, opinions etc. 'Life' became the closest definition of 'me' that I could comprehend. My name, my nationality, the roles I played or the things I do—those were all scout badges I collected along the way, none of which have any bearing on who I am. With or without them, I remain *me*.

The danger emerges when we get used to these badges, believing them to be a part of who we are. Also, these badges are not always material possessions. For example, the once-high flying executive may struggle with their identify during unemployment, 'I was used to being the top dog of the group,' one told me, 'and now I'm not.' Or in the case of ex-convicts reintegrating into society after a prison sentence. 'The hardest part is staying away from your old friends,' said one. 'For me to start a new life, I have to break away from everyone I know. But I don't know who I am without them.'

We lose ourselves when the things we've attained in this life leave us. And yet, they never belonged to us to begin with. The question of 'Who am I?' started to feel less fitting as my awareness of Life grew. Now, I prefer to refer to: *What* I am.

Like the ever-present sky, undamaged or changed by clouds and rain, the wisdom of Life was always there. I just got so caught up in the quest to collect badges that I lost sight of my true nature. I moved away from my personal power and assumed the belief that my value rested on everything outside of me: What my partner thought of me, how many glowing achievements were in my CV, whether I was the best daughter or favourite grandchild.

Don't get me wrong. There are incredible benefits of working towards goals in life. Achievements are powerful motivators that make life feel fun and exciting. The fine line lies whether we allow these things to define us.

We can start by examining our choice of words.

For example, a coffee drinker, who grows so accustomed to each morning's cup, begins to think they can't function without it.

Such an idea becomes so engrained, we start referring to it as part of our identity. 'I am a coffee drinker,' one might say.

This, however, is different to 'I drink coffee', as the former ties the self to the badge. The latter, on the other hand, recognizes the behaviour of consumption to be separate from the self. The difference would be the same as saying, 'I am a necklace wearer,' and 'I wear a necklace'.

Although just a minute difference in language, when we repeat such things—tens, hundreds, and thousands of times—we embed it deeply into our subconscious, and our bodies respond in alignment. At some point, we forget about a life before coffee, discarding the possibility of ever being without it. In fact, any threat that separates us from it is faced with grasping desperation to retain it.

I use coffee as an example because it is conceivable that one can, at some point, stop drinking coffee—even if they consider themselves an addict. Now, what if we consider the other types of 'coffee' in our lives—the places of belonging we have grown attached to?

'I *can't* move away because I *can't* leave my family,' a friend said to me once, turning down a dream job in another city. 'I *can't* leave him; I would have to start all over again,' the familiar lament from people desperately hanging onto relationships that died long ago. These limitations we enforce upon ourselves hold us back from moving towards our own life's adventure. We cage ourselves, then complain about not being free. We have hopes and dreams, then blame the world for not letting us fulfil them.

What have you ruled out as 'impossible' in your life?

What is the difference between *enjoying* a coffee and *needing* a coffee? What does *needing* do to *enjoying*? What happens when we grow used to the morning coffee, and one cup is no longer enough? (Hint: hedonic adaptation.) In our life, how much do we truly *enjoy* our metaphorical coffees, without the grasping attachment of feeling like we *need* it?

That emotional scene in a movie, where lovers say, 'I need you,' to each other, feels intense and full of love. However, how can you fully love someone for who they are, if there is something you *need* them to bring to your life?

Each time we say we '*need* something', we are unconsciously telling ourselves that we are not whole. We affirm that we are lacking something, and it can only be filled by that person, place, or thing. The more we reinforce it in our choice of words, the greater our attachment becomes. We mask it as belonging, but it turns into more of a desperate attempt to keep everything we *need* in place, exactly as we *need* it. If one of them slips off course—for instance, we are rejected by our community, or our relationship with our partner changes—we fall into a desperate spiral of trying to move it back where we *need* them.

Welcome to the trappings of the human mind. So, what can we do about it?

How do we remind ourselves that we were whole before our badge collection obsession?

If you're contemplating this, you are already in the process of bringing power back to yourself. Each time we consider this, we deepen our understanding. Each time we recognize that we are not the external places we belong to, it loosens its grip on us—just like moving memories into a mental furnace, deep attachments take repeated contemplations to dissolve. However, each time you do, you nurture the growth of your inner wisdom.

Your truth is not an acquisition of knowledge, but rather, a gentle unfolding from within. The more time we spend examining our nature in contemplation, the more we come home to our innate wholeness and the voice of our intuition grows louder.

I began to hold a very different definition of happiness. I refer to this as the difference between joy and happiness: the former is the temporary spurt of positive emotions we gain from achieving a goal or going on a holiday; the latter is sensing the power of our enduring presence—Life. It's there as you brush your teeth, tie your shoelaces, or tidy up after a day's work. If you give, even the simplest activity, your complete presence, you'll feel it.

Even as you read this book. Move your fingers so slowly over these words so that you can feel the texture of the page. Or if you're listening to this book, listen so intently that you hear the silence behind the words.

Do this for ten seconds.

Notice the difference you feel.

The simplicity of these practices means you can do them anytime, anywhere. Not only do you get a glimpse of Life, but you'll also build mental muscle for self-mastery—in short, taming your monkey mind.

So, next time your mind goes into your narratives of lack—your *need* for others to complete you, or your anger that what you *need* is not present—contemplate your wholeness before the badges. And if that's too hard, start with the simple practice of feeling the texture of what's in front of you.

To me, happiness now means connecting with Life and appreciating all the little things we take for granted: the knowingness that we are always whole. This happiness does not come from awards and accolades, and is not contingent on belonging to anyone or any place. It exists even when life doesn't go our way. Our connection to that happiness is always available to us.

Happiness is an inside job, and each time we deny this, we hand over the power of our life's control panel to others. It's not an easy concept to accept. It only takes a brief scroll on the internet to see the number of brands claiming that happiness is something to be acquired, or is a physical place. Come get a 'Scoop of Happiness,' says the ice cream store. Or 'A Slice of Happiness,' says the pizza man. And, of course, Disneyland: 'The Happiest Place on Earth'.

So, if you're not fully there yet, it's okay. Sit with it. If someone had told me this before I was ready, I would have laughed it off, and probably felt a strong urge to punch them in the face!

The only thing I invite you to do is contemplate, giving it space to marinate in your mind. Energy flows where our attention goes, and the more you tune in, the more you awaken.

When American singer-songwriter Nightbirde auditioned on *America's Got Talent* in 2021, she performed her original song 'It's OK'. She brightened the room with her vibrance, receiving the Golden Buzzer from Simon Cowell, all while battling cancer in her lungs, spine, and liver.[18]

'It's important that everyone knows I'm so much more than the bad things that happen to me,' she said. 'You can't wait until life isn't hard anymore, before you decide to be happy'. She died shortly after on 19 February 2022, at the age of thirty-one.

Whenever I think of Nightbirde, I am reminded of the preciousness of our human life, and how many of us spend it confined in the fixed models of how life *must* be—rejecting all other possibilities of how it *could* be.

I used to think that the only way to find peace with oneself was to break away from everything—exactly what I did during my sabbatical. However, while physical distance helps gain perspective, not everyone has the option to drop everything, run to the mountains, and lead a monastic life.

When we return to the intensity of our lives, it's easy to revert to habitual states of mind. As slow mornings return to 9 a.m.

inbox explosions and quiet reflections to endless errands, within the madness is where the real inner work begins.

If you're committed to coming home to yourself, if the system is no longer serving you, then you must put in the work. Notice the language you use with yourself, catch yourself when you slip, and correct yourself when you do. Slowly, but surely, you will reorient the neural networks you once had, and create a path that brings you towards the enduring happiness of Life. This will become your new habitual way of being. You need not be the monk in the woods to recognize your belonging to self.

If you can see your surroundings for what it really is, you can transcend it. However, if you get confused by it, then you will get lost in it.

At the same time, the happiness of belonging to oneself doesn't mean cutting off external places of belonging. Badges are nice, and there is nothing wrong with enjoying your coffee. It's about recognizing that neither of them define you.

This sense of self-belonging is the foundation of authentic connection. When we belong to ourselves, we're free to connect with others without depending on their validation. We can love others purely for who they are, for we no longer *need* them to bring us happiness. This freedom brings with it a pure, unburdened love—the one that flows without any fear of rejection.

Imagine entering any situation—at work, at home, with friends—without the need to mould yourself to others' expectations. Without feeling the need to explain yourself repeatedly, until they agree with your point of view or see you the way you think they should. With this unshakable belonging to self, we're no longer grasping to be perceived in a certain way, or to be affirmed. In this space, we're able to listen more deeply, see more clearly, and be *more* present. We bring the gift of our undistracted self, and in that state, everything sharpens—our decisions, our focus, our intuition.

Consider this at work. If we're no longer defined by our job title, our sense of belonging isn't bound to others recognizing or respecting us in a particular way. Instead of navigating relationships based on an unspoken need for validation, we're free to build genuine human-to-human connections. Our mind becomes uncluttered, and we're able to tune in, adapt, and grow in the flow of challenges and changes, rather than resisting them.

Now, think about home life. If we're no longer clinging to the notion of being a perfect parent or partner, or that our loved ones must treat us a certain way, our relationships become lighter, free-er, liberated from the weight of expectations. This freedom brings us closer. Our love for our children and partners become a space of acceptance, where they can fully show up as themselves, and you can embrace them as they are.

The psychological safety to show up in our natural state is the breeding ground for mutual flourishing. Instead of seeking the proof of their love through actions, you simply accept what comes. Everything becomes a blessing. In this state, you experience belonging as a choice, a gift, rather than something to be earned. It's an openness that fills your heart and enriches every connection you make.

Think about the coach-coachee relationship—not the kind of coach who tells you what to do, but instead, the ones that help you navigate yourself through powerful questions, helping you arrive at your own solutions. In such relationships, the coachee is offered a unique sanctuary—a place where they can show up without fear of judgment to do the brave work of facing themselves.

This experience is transformative because, unlike relationships that generally come with expectations and roles, a coach offers non-attached empathy, holding compassion without entanglement. Non-attached empathy means being present and empathetic, yet maintaining a space that allows us to see someone's challenges clearly without taking them on as our own. A coach is not of much help if they're in the ditch with the coachee!

The uniqueness of a coach-coachee relationship lies in our belief that people are naturally whole and resourceful. We believe that every coachee has an innate knowing of what they need to do, but it is overshadowed by the waves and waves of advice dished out each day. Our role as a coach, therefore, is to help them tap into their own voice and learn to trust it.

Consider how this relationship differs from the other relationships we hold, and how belonging can hinder our ability to hold open exploratory space for one another to grow in a way that is right for them. The community leader who wants us to stay within the confines of the group's traditions, or the parent who pressures their child to follow a certain career path to uphold family reputation.

Be it knowingly or unknowingly, much of the advice we are given is littered with the needs of the advice giver, even if they genuinely hold the desire for you to be well.

We are guilty of it ourselves. We want people to be well according to our terms, in the way we believe it will help them. We let our experiences be the benchmark of theirs.

Think about the passion-filled activity of venting. A wild tennis match with those who are excited to play, shooting through rounds of criticism that seemingly support the releasing of pent-up emotions. While it may feel satisfying in the moment, venting rarely leads to realizations and growth. A place where family and friends can unleash their full-blown expectations of how things should be, venting deepens the divide, reinforcing the I'm-right-and-they're-wrong, keeping us stuck in a flurry of emotions, rather than moving beyond it.

Think of all the times a friend went on and on about how much of an asshole her boyfriend was, where you added fuel to the fire by supporting her, but later, they ended up staying together. Your support offered temporary relief, but no real change.

Now, let's look at the other side.

Bring up all the times you vented about your partner to your friends and felt heard when they agreed with you. It was never really about 'problems' with the other person—they were reflections of the pain you felt from not getting what you *needed*, and your desperate desire to be loved the way *you think* you deserve.

After the high of venting dissipates, you're left, once again, missing the things you *should* possess, the things that are holding you back from happiness.

Compare this to non-attached empathy, the holding of open space where people can see themselves clearly, where the focus is not on the problem but the person who is experiencing it. Instead of 'How could they do that!', you might curiously ask, 'Why is this important to you?'

'Because they *should . . .*'

Oh? *Should?* According to whom?

By doing this, we begin to turn our attention away from the stimulus and turn towards our own self-enquiry to examine the root of our unhappiness. The spotlight inward reveals our uncomfortable truths—attachments, self-worth, the need for validation—the painful path of realizing that it was more about us than it was about them all along.

So, instead of trying to wrestle the world and pin it down, do the work in addressing your own clinging, striving, and inner disturbances. There is no perfect place of belonging *out there*, but if you do the work *in here*, what happens out there will have much less power over you.

When was the last time you truly felt seen? Even those closest to us tend to look at us through the lens of their own roles, perpetuating their existing perception of us.

'This is scary,' said a coachee once during our session. Intrigued, I asked, 'In what way?'

She continued. 'It's like holding up a mirror that forces me to see myself, and even though it's scary, I know I have to look.' She proceeded to share how rare it was to feel seen, *truly* seen, how people are constantly talking *at* each other, but never fully seeing each other.

Take a moment to reflect on the relationships you have with the five people closest to you. Do they fully see you? If the answer is no, then could it also be true that they don't feel fully seen by you either? How does it feel knowing that people closest to you might be hiding parts of themselves from you in fear of your judgement?

While it is useful to know there are safe spaces out there such as in the presence of a coach or therapist, I believe there is also room for us to redefine what it means to belong to one another, so we can bring this space of psychological safety into our everyday interactions. Imagine if you could offer the ones you love the chance to be fully seen by you. How much more meaningful that would feel than to know that the only place they feel they can be themselves is when they pay someone to speak to them?

What about me? you might be thinking. *What will I get in return? How can I make sure they will also fully see me?*

Good job! You caught your inner dialogue. The grasping mind that is driven by expectations of how others should treat us, and our inability to be happy unless we get our fair share. Now you've caught it, you have the power to rewrite it.

Let's expand our mind into the realm of possibility.

The ripple effect of a single human being is far greater than we can fathom. Imagine how different relationships would be, if we were willing to dive into the full spectrum of each other's humanness. When we listen, we do it with our whole heart, and not our head—knowing that steering off course is sometimes the necessary adventure to arrive at our own conclusions. If we could let people be the author of their own lives, knowing that we are responsible for our own healing and happiness. We stop suffocating people with our expectations and belonging begins to take on a whole new meaning.

Belonging becomes a place where we feel truly seen: accepted for our messy, unsure, and unfinished selves. Whether people offer that space to us is in their control; however, we can still choose to offer that space for others. If, instead of norms, traditions, and titles, we recognized one another for our complexities and contradictions, people around us could lay down their armour and let themselves be known.

What a world that would be, and the forging of that world starts now.

The next time you notice the urge to launch your inner advice monster at someone, ask yourself:

- *What assumptions am I making about this situation?*
- *How are my own experiences shaping the advice I feel compelled to give?*
- *What curious questions do I have that could help them explore their own inner world?*

Try simply holding space for them to share, without attempting to fix or direct their path. Encourage their exploration with, 'I hear you,' or 'Tell me more'. Reflect back words they said or emotions you sense.

This is your invitation to let them play in their own playground. When we become aware of how much we impose our world on others, we start to realize how little we listen and how little space we hold for others to be themselves.

We all have the ability to start changing right where we are, letting it ripple into the interactions around us. Happiness is the noticing of Life, the realization that the world, just as it is, and we, just as we are, are whole.

Consumption and attachments are the falsehoods we lead ourselves to believe that we need in order to be happy, yet our happiness is right here with us. If we practice catching ourselves each time we blurt out 'I am . . .', 'I need . . .', 'it must . . .', or 'it should . . .' and inquire into the validity of these statements, we confront the unconscious programming that tells us we are not enough and something more is always required. By spotlighting the subliminal messages we feed ourselves, we usurp the power to change them by choosing constructive statements that support the realization of our happiness.

As we challenge ourselves more and more, we awaken to how many of these 'shoulds' and 'musts' were implanted in us, long before we even had a choice to decide for ourselves. The way we believe relationships *must* play out, the roles family members *must* play, or the way that people *should* be treated—a list of rules that were handed over to us, accepted, but never challenged.

The more we reflect on the number of times we have felt judged when seeking support from those we belong to, we begin to replace our urge to give advice with the urge to offer space. The more we untangle ourselves from our conditioned responses, the better we are at allowing people to show up as their full selves. Each time we catch ourselves ready to launch into lecturing mode, ask:

- *Am I allowing the other person to grow on their terms?*
- *Am I supporting the emergence of their inner wisdom or am I attached to a fixed view of how things should be, which I'm now imposing on them?*

Every time we catch this and bring ourselves back, we train our mind. Over time, we begin to loosen our grip on our attachments. As we let go, we allow Life to emerge in ourselves and others: a place where we tune into the whispers of intuition and unburden ourselves from our badges. In this space, happiness flows naturally through us, no searching required.

The way out of the illusion, is in.

REFLECTING

Happiness is an inside job. There is a life force that resides in us all that is not dependent upon external possessions, roles, or achievements, and that life force is our beingness, the true essence of who we are. We call this Life with a capital 'L'. Happiness is commonly associated with our attachment to the external, when we gain more, when we achieve more, and we falsely associate our sense of self with these things, to the point that we don't believe we can be happy without them. This belief makes our identity a fragile construct, shaped by external expectations. However, we were whole, long before we started attaching 'badges' to our identity, we were whole then, and we are whole now.

If we have the bravery to create space between ourselves and our conditioning about how things should be, we can reclaim our personal power and transform our relationships. We can cultivate spaces for people to show up as their full selves. This freedom to be seen and accepted in our full complexity fuels the richness of genuine connection. In doing so, we rediscover our inherent wholeness and a deeper, lasting sense of happiness.

Ponder

- How do I define happiness?
- What would it look like for me to love someone without needing them to change or fulfil a particular role?
- How often do I use the word 'must', 'ought', or 'should'?
- What would happen if I embraced my full, unfiltered self, even in spaces where I usually conform to expectations?

Be Your Own Self Coach

Think about a time when you felt compelled to 'fix' or 'help' someone by giving them advice. What's driving this urge? Is it really for them to grow in their own terms or for you to impose your ideas about how things should be? The next time someone shares something with you, instead of jumping to offer advice, try just listening.

Notice how it feels to simply hold space for them. What happens when you resist the urge to 'fix' or provide an answer? What did you learn about them that you wouldn't have if you had launched into advice giving?

How does creating space to allow for yourself and others to show up fully evolve your understanding of happiness?

Chapter 5.2 – The Belonging-Happiness Situationship

We've been introduced to situationships already: a relationship that lacks definitive loyalty and commitment.

We explored this in relation to modern work engagements, framed under the pretence of 'family culture', when the landscape is now starkly different to the steadiness and loyalty we saw in previous generations.

Another interesting situationship is that between belonging and happiness. While I've shared my journey in discovering happiness, let's also take a look at the research on this topic.

Like many things in science, researchers rarely agree to a clear definition of a concept. Happiness is no exception. However, even as theoretical models of happiness and well-being span an array of perspectives, there are commonalities where the nature and dynamics of belonging play a critical part.

One of the most influential frameworks for understanding happiness is Self-Determination Theory (SDT) by Richard M. Ryan and Edward L. Deci.[19] This theory identifies three core psychological needs that, when met, set the stage for human flourishing: autonomy, competence and relatedness.

According to SDT, these intrinsic needs act as the foundation for a fulfilling life. When satisfied, we experience a sense of meaning and purpose, yielding enhanced motivation and well-being. Ryan and Deci recognized that 'the human spirit can be diminished or crushed', that we can 'reject growth and responsibility', describing the presence of these non-optimal states in the 'millions who, for hours a day, sit passively before their televisions, stare blankly from the back of their classrooms, or wait listlessly for the weekend as they go about their jobs.'

SDT offers insight into the design of social environments that support or hinder human well-being. While they don't specifically use the term 'happiness', the description of an ongoing sense of well-being, or 'eudaimonia', closely resembles the notion of enduring happiness.

They also touch on how it differs to temporary joy, highlighting how a 'focus on materialism' only provides 'fleeting satisfaction'.

What's interesting is the delicate balance between relatedness (the need for connection) and autonomy (the need to be true to oneself, that one's actions are self-determined), how happiness can be derived from being with others, but also from the freedom to be ourselves.

Relatedness refers to the feeling of being connected to others, that we are part of something greater than ourselves. It drives our search for belonging, the beauty of a shared purpose and togetherness, identified as a critical component in our well-being and happiness.

However, the need for relatedness may, at times, conflict with autonomy, as social conformity is often rewarded or *required* to maintain belonging. This means relatedness might compromise the fulfilling of one's autonomy. Our psychological need to feel that we are in control of our lives, that we can freely make choices that reflect our true self, can easily be at odds with societal expectations.

And hence, the situationship—belonging sometimes helps; yet, sometimes, hinders our pursuit of happiness.

When we belong to a group, it naturally comes with expectations encouraging us to take on certain behaviours, we might even take on those behaviours proudly. This is because the feeling of relatedness can sometimes be so good that we forget our autonomy altogether.

So, where does that leave us? Two needs that coexist but don't always come together.

While we inherently desire connection and relatedness, we simultaneously yearn to be our true selves. Perhaps, a starting point is to ask ourselves some questions:

- *Does my place of belonging celebrate my uniqueness?*
- *Does it support me to do what I want to do, even if it differs to the group?*
- *Does it embrace moments where I go against the grain?*
- *Does it allow me to express my authentic self?*

If the answer is yes, then your place of belonging seems to allow for both relatedness and autonomy, and you probably feel it too. If the answer is no, what impact is this having on you?

This simple step of acknowledging it is a gateway to grow beyond it—being both the experiencer and observer of your life.

How can we nurture our self-belonging? The more whole we feel with ourselves, the more we can offer non-attached belonging to others.

Consider this woman who chose her own life. Previously, she was following strict family expectations in fear of rejection. However, she began to rethink her life after a cancer scare. Against her parent's will, she married a man of her own choosing, which was outrageous enough for them to not attending the wedding. The sadness she felt on her wedding day made her realize the conditional relationship she had with her parents. 'They loved me if I played the part,' she said. 'But I knew I had to do it for me.'

She quit her job in finance and pursued a creative career. Now, in her forties, she has rekindled her relationship with her parents.

'For years, I lived for their approval. Then, I realized I'd never feel at home in my life unless I stopped living for theirs. Now, I still love my family and I'm very glad they're in my life again, but I don't need their permission to be me.'

We may not have good examples in our life to emulate, but we have every power to start the journey of walking home to ourselves.

Let's consider another prominent, yet very different theory of happiness: David Lykken and Auke Tellegen's Set-Point Theory.[20]

It suggests that 44 per cent to 52 per cent of our happiness is associated with our genetic make-up. Their research on a large sample of twins suggested that we all have a biological baseline we return to, even after major life events, both positive and negative. This is irrespective of our socioeconomic status, education, or religious commitments.

The participants ranged from those who didn't finish high school to those with PhDs; those who lived on farms and those who resided in large cities or moved overseas. They believed that people have a remarkable ability to adapt to their circumstances. Hence, unless an event was incredibly difficult, it did not 'seem to have lasting effects on one's mood'.

Before we hang up our hats and give up on our ability to make any difference to our happiness, remember we have another 48 per cent to 56 per cent in our control!

In the context of belonging, it can go both ways. If we build genuine meaningful relationships that supports the vibrancy of our being, it can positively impact the 48 per cent to 56 per cent beyond our biological baseline. This nurtures our relatedness. On the flipside, an obligatory belonging that quashes our being, or a belonging we pursue so intensely for the want of validation, can negatively impact our happiness. The slippery slope of belonging means we often start at the former and end in the latter, as bonds tighten, expectations naturally emerge.

It's a rare sight to encounter someone who seems truly free from attachment and expectations: like a wildflower growing untouched in the middle of a busy street. They move through life with a grace that feels almost foreign, unburdened by the weight of others' opinions or the pressures of success. There is an ease in their presence, a lightness, as though they are untethered, like a leaf floating effortlessly on a breeze.

If or when we meet someone like this, we can't help but wonder: Is this real? Or is it a carefully constructed defence mechanism that they've built to protect themselves from the world's demands? Are they truly happy or have they taught themselves to disconnect?

Our mistrust for such a way of life leads us to question ourselves: Is it really an impossibility though? Or are we just so used to relying on external sources of happiness that we feel thrown off in the presence of someone who has moved their focus within?

According to the Set-Point Theory, if a significant portion of our happiness is already out of our control, then it would make sense for us to go inwards, uncovering forms of happiness that is within our control first—before giving away all our power to external fluctuations.

For example, meaningful relationships are critical. However, whether they will continue to nourish and support us is out of our control. We may be familiar enough with relationships to know that regardless of how hard one party tries, if the other one gives up, the relationship fails. Therefore, belonging to people and places should be the icing on the cake—the dessert, not the main course. Our main course is the happiness we nurture from within, the fulfilment we find in self-belonging that makes sure we don't go hungry.

Beggars can't be choosers. If we want to have the power of choice in our lives, we must set ourselves up in a way that we aren't left begging. Our belonging to self, if cultivated first, is what will bring us sustainable, lasting happiness. The more we grow from a place of internal flourishing, the less we are at the mercy of how other people treat us.

The more we connect to the wholeness of Life, find peace and acceptance within ourselves, the less responsibility we place on others to make us happy, and the more empowered we feel to be authors of our own life.

If we only have 50 cents out of the dollar left, we better spend it wisely.

What does belonging to oneself look like?

We've all seen the live-love-laugh and gratitude memes floating around the internet. Do they work? Yes. Have they been backed by science? Yes. Have we seen it enough times that we are numb to hearing about it? Also, yes.

Therefore, I'd like to offer something a little more unconventional.

Give something away.

The popularized self-help idea of 'putting yourself first,' and 'you are the most important,' means that we often bring up the image of a spa day or retail therapy as a form of self-love. The idea of putting others first, or giving something away, may seem to be the worst way to achieve more happiness. It may sound counterintuitive, but it's one of the easiest ways to nurture authentic happiness. Moreover, it is completely in our control, and has science backing it up too!

In the frame of SDT, giving something away activates our competence and relatedness. Furthermore, if you give willingly—

and not because a book you read forced you to—you also fuel your autonomy.

Boom, there you go: all three psychological needs checked off!

So, whether it is lending a helping hand, buying coffee for the person in line behind you or offering a simple smile, every act of prosocial behaviour has a consistent and substantial link to increasing our own happiness.

Pablo Picasso once said, 'The meaning of life is to find your gift. The purpose of life is to give it away.'

Here is the intriguing part: It's not just about any type of giving. There is a nuance in how we do it. Direct acts of kindness, when you offer help to people face-to-face, has the most profound effect on your own happiness. Think of the difference between dropping a coin into a charity jar and sitting down to listen to a friend in need. One is a gesture, the other is a connection. Therefore, not all giving is equal! To avail the greatest boost of our happiness, the act of giving must be paired with an emotional exchange.

And it doesn't quite end there.

How we do it also matters. As mentioned, when we give freely, it activates our autonomy, making our happiness soar. This happens because we gain a sense of alignment between our actions and our true selves. So, when you're giving, give to whom you want to—it doesn't have to make sense to anyone else.

One day, I was out shopping with my partner. As we exited a popular mall, we caught sight of two people sitting on the street: one, an elderly lady selling single stem roses. Less than a meter away was, a beggar with one leg, holding what looked like a yoghurt tub with coins in it.

I instinctively reached into my pocket, dropped in a few coins into his yoghurt tub, and continued our way to the next shopping centre. A little while later, my partner asked me, 'Why did you choose to give it to the beggar and not the lady selling flowers?'

I paused to think. 'The beggar seemed like he needed it more.'

'Interesting,' he responded. 'I would have given it to the lady. At least, she was doing what she could to work for her money.'

I found his logic equally interesting; I had never thought of it. In this situation, we agreed there was no right or wrong logic, just different ways of thinking.

Coming back to autonomy, if I were instructed to give to the lady and not the beggar, that infringement on my freedom of choice would have impacted my autonomy, and hence my happiness in the experience. Likewise, if I were expected to help someone, it would've also eroded the happiness I stood to gain.

If this feels like a methodical way of using kindness for your own benefit, it is. Does it take away from the purity that giving must come with? Maybe. But does it do good for us and others in the experience? Yes. Does it allow us to generate our own happiness without waiting on others to give it to us? Yes. Does that in turn allow people to live more freely as themselves, in the absence of our attachment and expectations? Yes.

Furthermore, this boost of happiness, which comes from within, creates a positive feedback loop: The more we choose to give, the more we tend to keep giving. This, in turn, becomes a tool to sharpen our own happiness, unlocking greater emotional rewards when we give from a place of genuine care. The more we give, the more we receive—building happiness from the inside out.

Now, imagine what the world would be like if we all shifted our pursuit of happiness this way. If instead of rushing to the shopping centre to engage in more, endless consumption for temporary spikes of joy, people extended a helping hand to each other wherever they went. They connected with each other, smiled when they made eye contact with a stranger, and slowed down to see what they could give another to help them on their way.

How has our understanding of belonging evolved: from waiting for the right people to accept us, to knowing that the power has always been with us to write our own story.

There is something freeing about reclaiming control of our own happiness, versus waiting for the world to fall into place. It's never guaranteed that other people will be what we want them to be, that they will treat us the way we think we deserve. However, when you have that unshakeable belonging to self, if they do, that's great, and if they don't, that's fine too.

Just like Nightbirde, let's tap into our inner resource and active a direct and intentional path to our own happiness. Remember: It's a choice, not a waiting game. When we give, we don't wait for others to come through for us. We create happiness through our own actions, and in doing so, we are not seeking validation or approval, but rather expressing our authenticity, empathy, and desire to bring kindness to this world.

As we choose the 'how' and 'when' of giving, a profound sense of happiness emerges, knowing that we are the creators of our own reality.

This shift from waiting to giving also redefines what happiness feels like. Unlike a grasping, needy happiness that stems from a feeling of lack, it is an expansive, non-attached happiness that emerges from love. It transforms the idea of belonging from something externally dependent into something that is rooted in our own capacity to breathe life into.

Instead of feeling that our happiness is a product of others' actions or the dynamics of a relationship, we realize that we can light the flame in our own hearts. When we are no longer waiting for someone to complete us, or the right place of belonging to come our way, we move more fluidly to the rhythm of our own being.

Our happiness and our well-being has always been ours to cultivate.

REFLECTING

Belonging can nurture or deplete our happiness, depending on its nature. However, while nurturing relationships can be hugely beneficial to our happiness, they are inherently out of our control. Enter the idea of giving. When we give, we cultivate our own happiness. It taps into the three SDT psychological needs of autonomy, competence, and relatedness.

Ponder

- What is the difference between seeking and creating?
- When was the last time I gave something away?
- What do I need to release or let go of to fully step into a life that I create for myself?

Be Your Own Self Coach

What is one thing you can give today? It can be time, energy, kindness or resources. Give it away in a manner that feels authentic and aligned with your values. Give it freely, think of it like a social experiment with yourself. Notice how you feel before and after the act. How did it shift your emotional state? Do it again, and again, and again. Track your progress.

Beyonding

Send three surprise thank you messages to:

1. The person who changed your life and doesn't know it
2. The person whose small gesture of kindness lifted you up on a tough day
3. The person who is completely oblivious to their superpower

Tell each of them about the difference they made in your life, start the message with, 'I wanted to drop you a note to say thank you for . . .'

Notice how you felt while you wrote out the message.
How did it feel when you sent it?
How did it feel when you read their response?

Lastly, in the box below, rewrite your definition of happiness:

Chapter 6

CONTROL

As we unravel the mysteries of the mind, we come to realize how easy it is to get influenced in group dynamics: We stand frozen in a crowd when our hearts want to help; our perception of available support changes our stress response; we conform, trading our autonomy for harmony.

We mentally block out the notion that everyone will one day leave us, rejecting information that threatens our fairytale.

Yet, a profound truth exists: We can either float like a lost paper bag in the wind, or learn mental chi-gong and let the wind work for us.

The more we understand our mind, the better we can manoeuvre it. Our happiness and well-being are not granted by circumstances, and in calling back our power, we can unlock the ability to shape our reality.

Chapter 6.1 – Locus of Control

Imagine standing in the middle of a typhoon. The rain crashes against your face; your clothes flutter in the wind. But, instead of running around frantically and feeling like you're about to be blown away, you pause and ask yourself: What can I do?

With that, you realize you are not a victim in a natural disaster: You are, and have always been, the capable guide of your own life.

You lean down to pick up your belongings, taking them with you as you calmly move towards shelter. Once inside a nearby café, you settle in with your hot chocolate and marshmallow, listening to the howling of the wind as you sink into the sofa. A sense of contentment comes over you seeing the contrast between the wildness of what's going outside to the peaceful sanctuary indoors.

You may not be able to change the typhoon, but you can sure change where you watch it from. This is the essence of locus of control: the power we believe we have in steering our lives—regardless of external forces.

Locus of control is generally categorized as external or internal. Remember the friend who is constantly venting to you about their life? How it is always everyone else's fault but their own? They are perennially the poor victim, and everyone else has done them wrong.

This is what we call external locus of control: one's belief that their lives are governed by fate, luck, or others' actions. They are the passive receivers of their fate—helpless and powerless—with no control over their experience.

Now, let's consider a different scenario.

A sixteen-year-old girl is in her full-blown teenage rebellion phase. Disinterested in partaking in family events, she bursts out in anger for no apparent reason. She also skips classes at school, and blames her life's mishaps on her parents not buying her the car she wants. 'I hate you!' she yells out. 'It's all your fault!'

The only things she seems to care about are her friends and her popularity on social media.

Her concerned mother, looking for the situation to change, recognizes that there is only so much she can do. Instead of attaching herself to her daughter's rollercoaster, she pays close attention to her own well-being. She continues with her hobbies, talks openly about her challenges, and welcomes new perspectives.

While the two still engage in the odd screaming match here and there, the mother, for her own happiness, is fully clear about her responsibility—that her daughter is on her own journey. There are endless excuses one can give to be sad, but she wasn't going to choose that path for herself.

This is called internal locus of control: the perception that we are active agents, capable of influencing the outcomes of our lives—including how we feel. Just like no one holds the power to *make* us feel a certain way, we have no ability to *gift* happiness to anyone in pain—regardless of how desperately we wish it for them.

Coming back to language, each time we catch ourselves saying, 'You *make* me angry!' or 'You *make* me . . .', know that we are reinforcing the falsehood that something external can impose a feeling on us: external locus of control.

This common statement that we never think twice about strengthens our belief that our happiness is dependent on others. Like the separation of self and coffee drinking, sever the language that gives our control to others. Instead of saying 'You *make* me angry!' correct yourself and say, 'When you did . . . I felt angry'.

Now, anger is a choice of response rather than a relationship of cause and effect.

Our locus of control orientation shapes our attitudes towards everything. It is the mental agility and authority we offer ourselves, our perceived capacity to grow, change, and be the sovereign of our lives. Those with internal locus of control tend to experience greater levels of well-being, resilience, and healthier social relationships. Unlike grasping attachment, where we place our self-worth in the hands of others, healthy social relationships is about the willingness to hold space, understand, and accept another as they are. Building together from a starting point of wholeness.

Let's explore this.

What does 'steadiness' mean to you?

Oftentimes, when we explore 'steadiness', people consider its dependence on something to help them feel so: a job, peaceful family life, a loving partner, routine, a community of friends—essentially, all the pillars of life we are taught are necessary to feel steady.

Therefore, when we consider 'steadiness within ourselves', it can suddenly feel groundless and scary. Our attachment pattern might nudge us into believing that if we let go of something, we must attach ourselves to something else—replace lost love with love from another source, for example—the mental trap of believing we must be attached to something else in order to be whole.

Of course, moonlighting feels more comforting: finding a new job before resigning from your last or dating another person in secret, before you break up with your current partner. Always having *something* to lean on, so you never have to face the discomfort of what's in between.

What does that do for us, though? Jumping from one hamster wheel straight to the next, one emotional attachment straight to another.

Where is Life in this? The space for self-belonging, to connect with the power of what we are? For as long as our attention is directed outwards, in search for our next place of attachment, or in focusing on maintaining a current attachment, we are too distracted to gain awareness of our internal resources. Over time, it makes sense that we feel unsteady, without attaching ourselves to others, that we feel we are lost without external belonging, for we've never given ourselves the opportunity to practice balancing on our own two feet. We move through life like a man in his nineties: completely dependent on his walking stick to stand up.

Non-attachment can be frightening, yet this counterintuitive action is what strengthens our self-mastery. The-Eat-Pray-Love rediscovery of oneself often starts with crashing and burning, before we gain the steadiness to live intentionally.

If instead of running, we learn to stay, watch instead of avoiding, sink into the discomfort of tension, we will eventually uncover the melody of our own song. It'll be a tune only we know the beat to, an unchoreographed dance that moves from the rhythm of our heart. Slowly, you discover *your* space, free from the interjection of others—Life.

This lifelong practice, even when we get great at it, is like being the poised ballerina: seemingly in perfect balance, while constantly engaging in a series of micro adjustments. However, by then, we dance with the knowingness that we can hold our own. Having awakened a whole new set of muscles, we emerge with an authenticity that attracts healthy, mutual connections, based on inner grounding and shared values.

Compare this to the anxiety and sensitivity we bring to interactions when we believe the course of our lives is controlled by others or happenstance.

Imagine the fear that, at any moment, things could collapse, and we would have nowhere to go, with no ability to stand on our own. We jump at the slightest sounds, for it may be a signal that our stability is under threat. Constantly feeling on edge as we wobble from side-to-side, thinking that we would fall, unless someone catches us. We struggle to engage in meaningful, reciprocal relationships for we are too busy trying to make sure that we are validated. We launch into self-protection mode each time we sense a shift, automatically assuming that it is about us when it may have nothing to do with us. Operating with the belief that we are fragile, when we are expansive resourceful beings.

The more externally inclined our locus of control, the more unsettled we feel during times of uncertainty, and we feel more stressed.

On the flip side, the more internally inclined our locus of control, the greater our tolerance of ambiguity, and the more agile we are at adapting to changing landscapes. Internals are more likely to persevere in times of adversity, engaging in action when faced with difficulty, proactively seeking resources. This doesn't mean that internals are isolated beings who figure out life themselves; they are more likely to proactively seek social support. Internals view their relationships as resources, available for access if they wanted. This activation of the power of perception (perceived social support) means they are more resilient to stress or the influences of others.

If you're curious about where your locus of control lies, without going through a formal assessment, take a minute to consider how you perceive the comings and goings of life events. Bring up a situation in your life now where you are experiencing stress.

What is the reason for it?

Was your immediate answer to jump to a situation outside of you or was your answer in relation to something inside of you?

Is it your work, parents, children or someone else that is *causing* you stress, or is it a work in progress for yourself in understanding your own triggers and how you cope with stress? See the difference?

Even when we say, 'It *created* so much stress,' we form an arrow of causation from the event to ourselves. In doing so, we are more likely to position ourselves as victims or recipients of stress. The more frequently we use such language, the more we reinforce to ourselves that we are at the mercy of others.

It's not as simple as that though.

Locus of control operates along a spectrum. So, the next question could be, 'What can you do to alleviate the stress you are feeling?' Do you draw a blank because life is out of your control? Or does your mind immediately bring up actions you can take to change your situation?

Due to the level of control internals feel they have over situations, internals could overplay this strength, and end up trying to control the behaviour of others, meaning they may come across as more punitive and less sympathetic than externals.

It's not that simple, right? You probably also saw bits of yourself that fell into both internal and external orientations.

The purpose of this is not to become absolute internals or externals, but to gain awareness of the influences at play, and how we can catch and reorientate ourselves.

Instead of something *causing* you stress, consider this statement: 'When workload increases, it triggers me because I have an innate desire to always be perfect. As a result, I feel stressed.'

The linguistics of this statement creates a separation between the event and self. It recognizes that I am in control of my experiences, and I have engaged awareness of why I am *responding* with stress. A response is a choice, and the experience itself has no power in *causing* me to feel anything.

The difference between this type of internal locus of control, and that of trying to change the behaviour of others, is the stability of its core. We may believe we can control the behaviour of others, and we can try; however, we all know there is no guarantee people will change. Therefore, by grounding our internal locus of control in self-development, we focus on the only thing we can truly influence—ourselves. From here, we are not only reaping the benefits of internal locus of control, but also carving a path for self-discovery and transformation.

Instead of 'What can I do to change my environment?', we can consider the question: 'What am I doing to contribute to this?'

By asking this, we recognize our contribution to the situation that has resulted in the current outcome, affirming that we are creators of our world. Reclaiming power also means reattributing blame. It's easy to say we want to be the sovereign of our lives; however, it's also easier to play victim of circumstance, than to take ownership of what happens.

Our habitual ways of thinking, the roles we have assigned ourselves, and the language patterns we have grown accustomed to all contribute to our mindset and beliefs. Therefore, while these might seem like a play on words, or letting someone off easy when they must pay for what they've done, remember: The more we carry the residual energy from an experience, the more we allow it to control our lives—shaping our mood, perspective and narrative over time.

Chapter 6.2 – Reorientation

While research suggests our locus of control orientation is a relatively stable trait, it is capable of being cultivated. Locus of control stems from social learning theory,[21] meaning we learn it through observing the events around us, how people respond to those events, and from there, we form our own view on how much our actions affect our outcomes.[22]

Many of us are not conditioned towards agency or self-efficacy. Particularly in Asia, with harmony being praised over tension, our social learning conditions us to be humble, recognize the achievements of others before our own, and use the collective 'we', when referring to success before recognizing personal contribution. It is customary to profusely deny our success when spotlighted, struggling with wanting to be validated by others, while feeling intensely uncomfortable when we are acknowledged, particularly in front of others.

In a 2021 study, 82 per cent of participants admitted that they have hidden their success to avoid being perceived as a bragger.[23] Only the lone outlier would proudly stand up to say, 'Yes, it was me. I created it. Not by luck or by anyone else, but by myself. I made it happen.'

If someone does manage to say this, they would probably attract a lot of attention—mostly unfavourable. We might label it as bragging, but somewhere deep within, a tiny part of us may quietly wish to do the same. Most of us struggle with self-promotion and, in fact, only 50 per cent of employees feel that their manager gives them adequate credit for their work.[24] So, both ourselves and our environment tend to undersell us.

If the worldly feedback falls short in recognizing the causal relationship between our behaviour and its outcomes, it makes sense why so many of us feel we're at mercy of our circumstance, developing the belief that the only option we have is to take what we are given.

However, like all things, unlearning and relearning is possible. We don't fail if we don't quit, and while we may be used to a certain way of thinking, it does not preclude us from adopting a new mindset. As long as we have the will to bring the unconscious into the conscious, examine it, and start operating differently, our brains are able to adjust and create new pathways of being. We call this neuroplasticity.

One of the most fascinating demonstrations of unlearning was The Backwards Brain Bicycle by Smarter Every Day.[25] In this challenge, engineer Destin Sandlin wanted to see if it was possible unlearn the skill of bike riding. Such a skill, which most of us learn as kids, becomes so second nature that we never really unlearn it, even if we don't ride a bike for years. He even highlights the saying, 'It's just like riding a bike', referring to something we do with ease without needing to think.

So, can something like this really be unlearned?

The challenge started when he was given a bike with the handles swivelled around: a backwards bike. If he moved them right, the bike would veer left, and vice versa. What he thought would be an easy task proved tremendously difficult. He took the bike to universities and conferences, and surely enough, no one else could ride it either. 'If you have a rigid way of thinking,' Sandlin said, 'you cannot change that, even if you want to.'

However, the mindset of 'sometimes, you cannot change,' also means that sometimes, you can. And therein lies the challenge. After practising on his driveway every day for eight months, falling, getting back up, and hearing his neighbours laugh at him, suddenly, there was a shift.

'It was like I could feel some kind of pathway in my brain that was now unlocked,' he said. He began to ride the backwards bike, describing it like there being a 'trail in [his] brain', which he needed to pay close attention to, for otherwise he would, 'lose that neural path and jump back onto the old road [he] was more familiar with.'

Any slight distraction would throw him off.

The even more incredible part was when he set the same challenge for his son, who was able to achieve in two weeks what had taken him eight months. 'It's clear from this experiment that children have a much more plastic (flexible) brain than adults'. However, it's also clear from this experiment that it is also possible to rewire an adult brain—it just takes a lot more work!

After spending eight months unlearning how to ride a bicycle, Sandlin jumped on a normal bicycle in Amsterdam and . . . he couldn't ride it anymore! When laughed at by onlookers for twenty minutes, he continued trying. And suddenly, his 'brain clicked back into the old algorithm'.

Through this exploration of how we learn and unlearn, it confirms the difficulty of changing habitual ways of being, while also demonstrating how while difficult, it is still possible.

In the case of locus of control, we can move towards internality by acknowledging the causal relationship between what we do and what we achieve. We can start by exercising our muscle of self-promotion. Social learning teaches us that it could be seen as bragging, that it is not an attractive trait, and we are better off being humble and denying our achievements.

Yet, this learning has meant that we fall behind the few that dare self-promote, we make ourselves smaller to be socially accepted, unconsciously wiring in the belief that others' approval defines our worth more than our own acknowledgement. By self-promoting, we take control over how we perceive ourselves, and in showing up in our full power, we influence the perception others have of us too.

In 2016, Anna Vainer launched a movement in Google called #IamRemarkable.[26] Its mission is to help people speak more openly about their accomplishments. It started as an internal workshop, and soon expanded to the public.

As of December 2024, the initiative has reached over 670,000 people from 180 countries. Through a self-reflection exercise, it pushes people to take ownership of their achievements, recognizing how each of us have been remarkable in achieving incredible outcomes in our life. It involves practicing self-promotion—to ourselves, and in front of a group.

As an #IamRemarkable facilitator, I have been moved to tears on many occasions, watching people struggle with discomfort, before finding the courage to celebrate themselves. It's common for people to say, 'I never realized how capable I am until I looked back'.

'I am remarkable because I am kind, even when the world isn't,' said one participant.

'If these [the achievements he wrote down] were other people's achievements,' another participant added, 'I would totally tell them to own it. But for some reason, when it comes to myself, it's so difficult to say it was me, even though I know it was.'

To sit with people in that tension is a gift, and to watch people weave through the discomfort is akin to watching a butterfly struggling in its cocoon before it finds its way free.

Owning our achievements is an honouring of the gifts that Life has given us. It is not a rejection of society to stand out. But if it risks our belonging to a group, then it says something about that place or situation. To flourish is our own responsibility, and if we're going to camouflage ourselves, then it is only natural to feel like we're just going along with life: a meaningless exercise driven only by the fact that everyone else is doing it. Social proof is a strong force of influence, and being led by it is as easy as riding a bike.

So, if you are starting to wake up to the bias of your surroundings, go grab a glass of water, splash yourself in the face, and give yourself a good shake. Riding a backwards bike won't be easy, but you'll gain a heck more control over your life than if you just kept going.

Pay attention to the words we connect to.

'We accept you for who you are,' may feel comforting, but the more important question is, 'Do *you* accept you?' If you are easily wooed by the embrace of others, allowing it to sweep you up like a damsel in distress, then ask yourself: What power am I giving away?

Grab a pen and paper.

1. Write down three traits about yourself you admire
2. For each traits, write down what difference you have made in the world because you possess this trait, no matter how big or small
3. Notice the effort that went into making these things happen
4. Say each one out loud, celebrating yourself for what you have done
5. Feel the gratitude in your body

Irrespective of whether anyone else accepts or celebrates you, make it a habit to celebrate yourself! If it feels weird or awkward, that's great. It's a sign that you're trying something new!

We are all remarkable, and each time you manage out an uncomfortable sentence of self-promotion, know that you are cultivating your belief in personal agency and self-efficacy. Each time you own your achievements, you pivot the focus from external factors to your own efforts and contribution. If you slip up, that's alright—make a mental note, and move on. You can also give those moments a name. For example, you might call it 'giving away', short for 'giving away your power'. By labelling it, you make it easier to identify the next time it arises.

One day, you may become so sick of 'giving away', you reach a point where you decide enough is enough. *Today is the day I take back control and stand for me*, you might tell yourself. And this will be the day that the force of your will overpowers your excuses.

Click. Did you hear that? That was your brain clicking into the algorithm of this backward bike.

The rules of the world are not set in stone; they can be bent, reshaped, and remade. The words we say, and the thoughts we think, translate into actions that either accept the control of others or claim control for ourselves. Social learning may have downplayed our capability, but there is no need for us to perpetuate these limiting beliefs. Ordinary is a setting on a washing machine, not a state of human flourishing.

Remember that time you looked at someone and thought, 'What a shame! They have so much potential. Only if they . . .'

Now, take that statement, and know that someone has said that about you—maybe you've even said it about yourself—and know that whatever force pulled you into accepting a smaller version of yourself, requires an equally powerful force to break you out!

If you operated at only 60 per cent of your capacity in this life, what would you say to yourself on your deathbed? How would the resourceful you, knowing what you know now, respond to the you that says, 'But I had no choice'?

I'm all for being gentle with yourself. However, there is also a time and place for self tough-love. This is not to be confused with self-deprecation and sinking into a spiral of self-blame, but it's the forceful nudge where you say to yourself, 'Come on, you know better so you can do better,' topped off with a smile of 'I believe in you!'

Growing up, I was part of the school's swimming team. When I think about my coach, he was someone who really pushed me to do my best. I was neither the strongest in my team, nor someone born with webbed feet. And yet, he never accepted any of my excuses—he was so tough on me! One time, he even said, 'I want to see you swim so hard, you vomit. And until you do, you're not getting out of this pool!'

Okay, I'm going to do just that, I thought, with a mixture of annoyance at him and frustration with myself. *Then you'll have to watch me have a heart attack and die, after which you'll know I wasn't cut out for this!*

Then, of course, I'd realized I could do it, after all. But it took a strong dose of tough love.

His toughness stemmed from a place of belief. His words kept me going. 'Judy, you trained for this. You can do better than that!'

He saw my potential to do better and was determined to coax it out. The training itself was gruelling, and it never felt easier. However, it soldered the belief in me that if we exercise, be it our physical or mental muscle, we will get better.

This is the mindset one must take on, when showing ourselves tough love. While having access to a coach is great, we are all capable of coaching ourselves too.

Every time we sense that an unresourceful state of mind has crept in, giving away our power to others, ask yourself:

- *What is happening inside me?*
- *What triggered this emotion?*
- *What filter am I seeing this experience through?*

Reorient yourself internally. Make your way through this tension by asking: What is it trying to show me?

Then, show yourself some tough love. 'What excuse am I giving myself right now? What truth am I avoiding?'

You make the choice: Are you going to let it consume you, or will you affirm your strength, your worth and navigate out of this experience?

If you feel muddled in it all, reach out to an outlier! Just as that participant said in #IamRemarkable, we are often better at identifying the extraordinary in others than in ourselves.

You may ask them the following questions:

- *In your view, what am I naturally talented at?*
- *What would you consider to be my strength?*

Ask them to provide examples and reasoning too. But remember: while they can shine a light on your capabilities, the work for you is to own it. So, instead of shying away and denying it, feel the discomfort and own it. Thank them, offer your gratitude for them helping you identify your power, then speak it out loud and repeat it back to them. Accept it and celebrate yourself. Always remember: They can aid you in your growth, but they can't do the growing for you.

Watch yourself in this process, and look out for thinking traps.

- *How come I'm not progressing as quickly as I want to?*
- *Why am I not as good as others in doing this?*

Our age, nationality, religion, culture, or life experiences will affect our locus of control predisposition. However, reorientation is not a comparison of starting points or the speed in which we can pivot.

Like the degrees on a compass, there is no 'right' direction, as it depends entirely on where you are going. You know the map of your own territory, and the angle required for you to get there. We all have a compass in our hearts; we just get lost after becoming conditioned to follow other people's directions.

So, if you *think* you don't know where to go, it's not that you actually don't know. The problem is we believe that the way to know is by *thinking*. Stop *thinking* and start *connecting*, not with others, but with yourself.

It's right there.

REFLECTING

Locus of control refers to the extent we feel we have control over our lives. It is broadly categorized as external or internal.

Externals feel the outcomes of their lives are determined by factors outside of themselves, be it another person or fate. For externals, their stress is the *cause* of an outside force, while for internals, it is a gateway for self-discovery and greater self-understanding.

An internal, on the other hand, might ask themselves, 'What is it about this situation that triggers me? Where did that come from?'

Internals have been linked to better well-being, greater adaptability, and resilience. While it is easier to blame others for the happenings in our life, there is freedom to be gained from taking ownership of our experiences. While locus of control is a relatively stable trait, it is a mindset that can be cultivated.

Ponder

- When you experience stress or frustration, what do you usually attribute it to? Is it something outside of your control, like the actions of others or external events, or is it connected to your own beliefs, expectations or behaviours?
- What language do you use when describing your challenges? Do you say 'I can't' or 'I have no choice' or do you say, 'I can learn from this'.
- Do you feel like a victim of your circumstances or an active participant in shaping your reality?

Be Your Own Self Coach

Becoming aware of, and changing the words we say to ourselves can be a powerful way to strengthen internal locus of control. The words you use alters the thoughts you think and hence the decisions you make and the feelings you feel. Start catching yourself when you say the words in the left column and replace them with the words on the right:

When you catch yourself saying…	**Say this instead…**
I can't	I choose not to
This happened to me	I responded this way
I have no choice	I have options
They made me feel	I allowed myself to feel
That's just the way I am	I can change that behaviour
I am so overwhelmed	I'm going to handle this in smaller steps
I failed	I learned

Beyonding

Create a representation of something you care about. It could be stick figures, a symbol, ball of scribbles, or an image from the internet. As long as it connects with you, it's fine. Represent it in colour, shape, and size rather than words. Create something that takes less than five minutes to complete.

Something I care deeply about...

Connect with the emotions of what you have created. Then, turn the page over for what to do next.

Cut out the picture you just created.

Ready? Time to create some chaos. Holding your picture, close your eyes and randomly tear the paper into three to four pieces (no peeking). If it feels uncomfortable, good—it's supposed to.

Open your eyes and look at your now fragmented picture. This torn up picture symbolizes the disruptions of the world—sometimes, the things we care about get torn up by external forces (although, this time, it was played by yourself).

Now, reassemble the pieces. You can stick them together if you have tape handy, but if not that's okay, you can piece them together on a table. You can line them up perfectly, overlap them, or even add more to it. The key point is to make it your own—whatever is meaningful to you.

Reflect on how you felt being able to repair, recreate, re-imagine, and redesign it into something new.

Even when circumstances out of our control tear us up, instead of focusing on what we cannot change, focus your attention on your creative power to re-shape your story.

Chapter 7

COURAGEOUSLY ALONE

We've probably heard the saying, 'Alone doesn't mean lonely'.

Being courageously alone means stepping into the uncomfortable realm of facing ourselves. We live in a world that reinforces fitting in, but there is a difference between fitting in and belonging. The former means you're accepted for what you do, what you give, or how you follow the crowd. It's about being part of something, but it's a hollow connection—a façade built on conformity.

On the other hand, belonging is not about what you offer, but who you are—just as you are. The truth is, most people never find self-belonging, because most never dare to break free from the chains of fitting in.

If we can accept that our unique path was never supposed to look like anyone else's, then the work of being courageously alone will reveal more than anything we'll find in a crowd. You will be misunderstood, people will look to you with disapproval, and the silence of solitude may be frightening, but in that space, you'll uncover the raw, unfiltered version of yourself.

The day you stop fitting in is the day you start living your truth. And when you realize it, you will never be afraid to walk alone again.

Chapter 7.1 – Fitting in ≠ Belonging

My first memory of 'belonging' was in 1994. I was five years old. My father had decided to move us from a small town called Tainan, in the south of Taiwan, to Sydney, Australia. My brother was only two months old, and no one in my family, barring my dad, spoke a lick of English.

On my first day at school, I sat in the back of the class, listening to my teacher and other kids. My mind drew a blank. It was a strange and almost outer-body experience, where I felt I was observing the room, rather than being in it. I could fade into the wallpaper and disappear, and no one would know.

I didn't mind it, though. The teacher smiled and nodded at me from time to time, acknowledging my existence. Everything was okay, until it came time for us to be given homework.

As the teacher handed out sheets of paper of English words, I panicked at the sight of seeing unfamiliar letters. However, I also felt at ease, as they looked easier than the Chinese characters I was familiar with. Although I didn't understand the instructions, I figured we had to write out the words over and over in the boxes below.

The lunch bell rang and the classroom emptied in an instant, as all the kids dashed out for lunch—all of them, but me. I didn't have friends and, as until that point I had yet to utter a word, it didn't surprise me that they never spared a second thought for the new Asian girl.

After the teacher unsuccessfully tried to converse with me, presumably to ask me to leave the room, she gave up, switching off the lights as she walked out.

So there I was—sitting by the window where the light filtered through, with my eyes tracing my classmates playing outside. I decided to do my homework. What else could a studious little girl with no friends do with extra time?

I pulled out the sheet of paper with unfamiliar symbols, took out a pencil from the case my mom had packed for me that morning, and began to write. As Chinese characters are written vertically, instead of writing the word 'CAT' horizontally, I proceeded to write C C C C C C C, all the way down the page until I reached the end. Then, I continued with A A A A A A, and T T T T T T T.

Just as I was reaching the end of my page, I felt the whip of a long thin shoelace catch the top of my arm.

'Ouch!' I instinctively grabbed my arm tightly in response to the sting, looking up to catch the smirk of a girl who was much bigger than me. She had short blonde hair, bright blue eyes, and freckles that ran across her cheeks and nose.

She said something to me, pointed at my page, then whipped me again. I don't remember how long it went on for, but only how confused and helpless I felt. When it finally stopped, she turned around and ran off. My heart kept pounding with a mix of fear, anger, and confusion.

A few minutes later, she came back—this time with the teacher. I was relieved to see the teacher, although that relief was short lived as the shoelace-whipper motioned for her to look at my work.

Now, they were both towering over me. The teacher's demeanour was of stern disapproval, while the shoelace-whipper pointed at me with a sneer of satisfaction as she reveled in my distress.

It was long after the incident I realized that I was 'dobbed on' (told on) for cheating on my homework, because I was writing each letter individually (as you would in Chinese) rather than as a full word.

I spent the next twelve months adjusting my rhythm to theirs: switching my noodles for ham and cheese sandwiches, unlearning Chinese because it wasn't 'cool' to speak another language. I even started introducing myself as, 'I'm from Taiwan, but I don't speak Chinese,' so I could dodge any potential ridicule.

Soon, I developed a witty sense of humour. It was a way to protect myself. If anyone was going to say something mean, I made sure I had something meaner to say in response! I wanted to strip myself of everything I was before I moved to Sydney, so I could be like everybody else. On the outside, I did a pretty good job. Eventually, my English surpassed my Chinese, and I learned to deflect the punches, even throwing a few back.

Strangely, as the observable differences dissipated and I started to act like every other Australian kid, I felt even less seen. It was like holding onto a secret you didn't want to hide, but lacked the capability of sharing.

In fact, I didn't even know what it was: All I knew was that I was still different. So, while the sting of the shoelace was long gone, the feeling of invisibility became ever more present. Before I knew it, I was fighting my way into a world that seemed just out of reach.

This is a familiar feeling for many Third Culture Kids. And as time went by, I learned the art of being a chameleon: switching my Australian and Taiwanese sides on and off, depending on what the situation required. It was like playing a game only I knew I was playing. Over time, I got so good at it that it became second nature. My accent would shift depending on the crowd: from British, to American, to Taiwanese.

'Why are you trying so hard to fit in?' someone once asked. 'You know it's weird that you change your accent to speak like them.' I remember responding with laughter; I found it hilarious because I hadn't even realized I was doing it.

Now I know this is called code-switching—switching languages, dialects, or communication styles depending on the social context, driven by the need to reduce social friction.

At the workplace, I've seen Singaporeans switch effortlessly between Singlish and English, depending on who they were speaking to. If they were with a fellow countryperson, Singlish offers a level of closeness that English can't, because it breaks the rigidity of corporate professionalism. On the other hand, if they were with foreign colleagues, English was used. 'It's just a social expectation,' one of them told me. 'I guess it's also a perception about professionalism.'

I got so good at code switching, I would subconsciously merge them in mixed groups. At a recent leadership workshop with Australians, Malaysians, Singaporeans, and Thais, I overheard some participants talk about me in the pantry.

'She is so Thai,' said one of the Thai members.

'Really? Nah! She is so Aussie!' replied the Australian.

You know you're fitting in well when people start sharing their racist views with you, about your own race, expecting your agreement.

One time in high school, while I was working in retail, a colleague of mine said, 'Oh, those damn slap faces [presumably referring to the flatter Asian features]. Always looking; never buying!'

'You know I'm Asian right?' I shot back.

'Oh, Judy darling,' she swiftly replied, completely unbothered by the fact that I just called her out. 'Not *your* type of Asian.'

Times like these showed me that I had fit in so well, that I had, somehow, moved out of their categorization of 'Asian'. The weird part? That's what I had always wanted as a child. However, the shock I felt from hearing them speak about Asians helped me come to a clear realization: You can master the art of fitting in, but it has nothing to do with belonging.

Thank you, ex-colleague, for accepting me as one of your own. But no, thank you. I'll stay in this limbo space of in-between, where I belong to myself and need not be categorized as neither here nor there.

It used to bother me. But over time, I started to realize that we all generalize and makes assumptions. Fearing social reprimand, we conceal our thoughts in public, but in places we think we are around like-minded people, those thoughts leak out. As a Third Culture Kid, people often mislabel you as one of their own.

You fit in so well, people forget how different you are from them. Marcus, a German, who grew up in Asia during his formative years, continues to speak German perfectly. 'I speak English with a German accent and no one believes I ever left the country when I tell them. I guess I'm not gifted linguistically,' he says jokingly—he acts and sounds German in every way.

However, his unseen operating system is completely different. 'It's pretty much like being a spy—minus the cool gadgets, action-hero status, and private jets.' he says. 'I have sat in meetings where people have said some outrageous things, things they definitely would not have said if they knew where I was from.' When I asked him if he said anything in response, he replied, 'Sadly no, but I really should have.'

While some chameleons are easier to pick out, others can be right in front of you and you'll never know.

Born from transient environments and loose emotional ties, the feeling of being a Third Culture Kid comes with a freedom that is both unsettling and exhilarating. Your identity is fluid, and you accept that everything around you will change. You move more freely through the world, shaping a unique kind of bravery, because you learn early on that you never fully belong anywhere, so there is no single set of expectations that can bind you.

I remember the look of shock horror on my mom's face when I told her I was going out with her, shortly after I had double eyelid surgery. My eyes were swollen like golf balls, and I had six big stitches on each eye. Deep shades of blue, green, and purple bruising all around. 'You can't do that! What if people see you!' she exclaimed. 'It's fine mom, people don't care,' I replied. And with that, I slipped on my shoes and went out. I remember the intriguing glances from onlookers, the kids that gasped and turned to their parents.

Whether it was for a few seconds, or at most a couple minutes, one thing was for certain: people care in the moment; then, they move on.

People are too consumed by their own lives to keep you lingering in their thoughts. We think that people talk about us all the time, when actually we occupy 1 per cent of their thoughts, while the other 99 per cent is on themselves. We're the main actors in our lives just as they are in their own. So, you might cross their mind for a split second; but soon, they will return to thinking about themselves.

Aman is an Indian Muslim, born and raised in Taiwan—a minority within a minority group. His mother tongue is Mandarin; although he also speaks English, as he went to an international school. His parents moved the family over from Myanmar, in hopes it would offer the kids a better life. While it naturally meant he would gain an understanding of the Taiwanese way of life, they still took every effort to ensure he retained his Islamic traditions.

'There was so much cultural conflict,' Aman told me. 'While my parents tried hard to teach us our traditions, trying to explain all of it to my Taiwanese friends was so tiring. They couldn't understand why I was forbidden from eating certain things, or why I had to leave activities halfway to pray.'

This pressure of having to abide by Indian Muslim customs, while fitting into the Taiwanese culture, meant he was constantly torn between two ideologies that were often at odds with each other.

'I would come home guilty every day, feeling like I had done the wrong thing,' Aman said. 'At that time, I believed what was taught at home to be the right thing.'

Not having anyone to talk to about it, life felt lonely—not because his friends weren't willing to listen, but because how difficult it was for him to explain something so complex and different to what they could comprehend. This feeling of loneliness wasn't just felt in Taiwan. 'Whenever I'd meet my family overseas, I still felt like the odd one out. I don't speak the language as fluently as them, and they don't understand my sense of humour. Because of this, I've never felt a desire to connect with them,' Aman said.

Splitting himself into two personas became his life. There was the Indian Muslim Aman at home, and the Taiwanese Aman that hung out with his friends. He pulled out the local dialect with swag, surprising people on a daily basis who assumed he was a tourist. He would make a reservation over the phone in perfect Mandarin and confuse the restaurant owners when he showed up.

His efforts to find belonging led him into troubled social circles. After being caught on CCTV at a bar fight, Aman found himself in prison. That marked the turning point of his life.

He remembers walking in on his first day and immediately knowing that he didn't belong there. 'I thought I was a badass, but that place is something else,' he says. While the inmates fought to gain dominance over one another, he kept his head down and did his chores . 'I always looked neat, shirt tucked, hair combed.'

Surprisingly, an inmate, who had been sentenced to life in prison, became his mentor. 'He [his mentor] said he had seen many people come and go, but he took one look at me and said, you don't belong here.'

It was behind bars that Aman began the difficult journey of coming home to himself.

Through processing his inner tension of being a *nobody*—for he didn't fit neatly in any circle—what emerged was an awareness that in the space of nowhere, he could be anything: an identity that was uniquely his own.

'I married Lucy, who is a Mormon. According to my tradition, she must convert to Islam. However, she is still a Mormon,' said Aman. 'I told her to convert *only* if she wanted to; it was not a compulsion. It made no difference to me. Life is messy enough already, and I saw no need to add another layer of complication.'

'My dad tries to be very open-minded,' he said. 'But he isn't, and that's okay. I've made peace with that. He has a right to be him, and me to be me.'

Having spent his life trying to meet everyone's expectations, it took a great deal of courage for Aman to challenge his deeply ingrained family traditions. 'Of course, I wanted my parents to be happy,' Aman said. 'Otherwise, I wouldn't have worked so hard to fit their expectations.' But he realized that his duty to himself was more important. It was to 'build a life that was right for him and his family (his wife and kids).' At the end of the day, no one is going to take responsibility for your life. So, following tradition for the sake of tradition is like believing that people long gone—who never met you—somehow know what's best for your life better than you do. He wanted to show his children that there is always an alternative beyond tradition, and when there are conflicting ideologies, there is every possibility for a new pathway to emerge.

'You have to believe in something greater than yourself,' he said, referring to his children. 'We challenge the system, not just for our own self gain but to be an example for our children, showing them that nothing is fixed and we will always try to do better'. His courageous move away from tradition was a way of inspiring his children to continue imagining, creating, and exploring—for anything is possible.

'I don't go to the mosque anymore,' he said. 'I felt it was all for show. It was more like a gossip-fest for aunties to congregate and talk about other people than a place of worship. I needed to find my own understanding and relationship with God. That's what is important to me.'

When asked what words he had for his younger self, Aman replied, 'Just believe in God, whichever God you choose. We're all guided.'

'Do what you want to do, eat what you want to eat,' he said. 'Life is short, don't spend your time struggling to fit in. You are also not the only person who feels different—other people feel it too. Be proud of who you are, as this pride will turn around everything in your life. Too much self-talk will keep you in a constant state of struggle. A lot of people will try to give you advice, as everyone feels they know everything. Yet, everything goes by, and only you can uncover the purpose of your life.'

As the world grows more interconnected, the rise of Third Culture Kids is reshaping what it means to belong. No longer bound by fixed ideals, their identities are the merge of a multitude of cultures, with each piece carrying its own values, traditions, and expectations. There is an absence of a clear, singular 'home' or cultural guideline, and the more it is imposed on them, the more it can leave them drifting in an endless sea of conflicting views on how to live, and who to be.

As the in-betweeners of this world, perhaps they are the outliers who help us see beyond fixed realities. If we feel trapped living up to the expectations of traditions, perhaps they can help shed light on things they have seen on their journey. They have the natural ability to move within diverse spaces, bringing forth alternatives that may not be immediately apparent. Unbound by inherited scripts, Third Culture Kids show us what it looks like to embrace complexity, hold contradictions, and remind us that we can have an identity beyond belonging to a singular dimension. They are the outliers who bring a lived understanding about the infinite ways to live this life, and their presence challenges us to question our fixed ways of thinking.

For all the places we say we belong to, is it *really* belonging? Or are we simply fitting in—albeit very well. What might it feel like to belong fully to ourselves? Moving beyond the narrow lines is not a forfeiture of what we have, but instead, an expansion. We can embrace the richness of our culture without being bound by it, and to be courageously alone means to illuminate a way of life that honours both individuality and interconnection.

So, what's the decision? Are we going to sit and sulk about how no one sees us and how lonely we feel? Or will we take it as permission to charter our own lives? Just because you fit in doesn't mean it equates to belonging, and it doesn't take being a Third Culture Kid to experience that. Your tenure in a community doesn't make it a death sentence. Befriend a Third Culture Kid, let their in-between perspective help you explore beyond yours. If you don't feel seen, don that invisibility coat, and fly the heck out of there! I can't guarantee what you will find, and that's the exciting part.

Let your curiosity for what lies beyond guide you, and as you move further away from others' expectations, listen to that voice inside and move closer towards yourself.

When faced with disapproval when you decide to change course, ask yourself: Are they coming from a place of pure intention and love for you? Or is it coming from their own fear of straying from the crowd? If it is the former, listen in and share with them your love. If it is the latter, let them be. Your timing need not be theirs, and smooth seas never made skilled sailors.

I once had a manager apologize to me months after a salary negotiation conversation. I didn't think anything of it at the time. I was clear about what I wanted: no added niceties, just a list of evidence I felt formed a strong argument. I got what I asked for, and it was a while after starting my new role that she picked up this conversation with me. 'I was taken aback by how clear you were about what you wanted, and my immediate instinct was to deem that behaviour rude,' she told me. *Oh yea?* I thought, bracing myself for what she was going to say next. 'Then, on reflection, I realized it had stemmed from jealousy. I was jealous that I could never show such bravery to do that for myself.'

That day, I learned that the feedback we get from people is more often a reflection of how they feel about themselves than about us. I admired her courage in sharing it with me, and it inspired me to do the same for others when I inadvertently box people into my model of the world.

Remember: If paving your own path were easy, then it wouldn't be called 'courageously alone'. And if fitting in was the key to happiness, then breaking free would never feel so profound.

REFLECTING

Adapting well or fitting in does not necessarily equate to belonging. Third Culture Kids are examples of people who may feel unseen despite fitting in well. The internal struggle of these invisible outliers are exasperated when we attempt to simplify complex identities, often in an effort to help them feel a sense of belonging.

These outliers have the potential to bridge diverse worlds, and if we could highlight their complexity rather than quash them, we give ourselves the chance to learn from them as a way of expanding and going beyond our own understandings of the world.

Ponder

- How do you distinguish between moments when you are 'fitting in' versus truly belonging?
- Where do you feel most accepted for who you are, without needing to adjust?
- When have you felt most disconnected with yourself? What were you trying to achieve in that moment?

Be Your Own Self Coach

Run through a day in your head as an observer of yourself rather than the experiencer. What beliefs or inherited scripts about life do you use? Where did they come from? If you had a sanctuary within, whereby these scripts would not exist, what qualities or values would be present?

If you know a Third Culture Kid, approach them with your inherited scripts and ask them to share with you the multitude and possibly conflicting perspectives they hold about it.

Chapter 7.2 – Breakthrough

In May 2022, I gave away 90 per cent of everything I ever owned.

I invited people over, and offered them to take anything they liked. My clothes, bags, art, electronics, furniture, decorations—anything they wanted—was theirs to take. My apartment was stripped down to bare white walls and one grey couch, what my friend described as 'sterile, cold, and surgery-room like'.

'Can you at least get a plant?' someone asked me. 'It kind of freaks me out to be in your place.'

To take it a step further, I decided to box up the few remaining things and started living life out of a suitcase—one medium-sized blue check in luggage.

This meant one pair of black pants and jeans, one work skirt, one of each essential item I needed, and nothing more. Flip flops became my go-to shoes for most occasions, and I had one pair of black flats and heels for work and other outings. All this while, I was the Head of Learning & Development at a UK-listed company, leading a regional team across APAC.

When people think of nomads, they often get the picture of a social influencer, yoga teacher, or crypto trader living in Bali, working from a café or some cool coworking space. I was quite the contrary: a corporate leader travelling across the region, developing teams, conducting workshops, and coaching leaders. From a professional perspective, I was just like anyone else you'd see in the office. However, while people went home after work,

I went wherever I was staying that day: hotel, friend's couch, or the place I was housesitting.

I had already been travelling a lot for work, so being in different places was not new. But there was no more counting down the days until I got to go home. That feeling of 'Ahh! It's good to be home,' when we open the door, or that blissful plonk when your head hits *your* pillow in *your* house no longer happened. I gave myself two months to see what I would learn.

But . . . why?

Contrary to what many people thought, I wasn't struck by a traumatic event that left me wanting to escape my life. Remember my search for happiness on my sabbatical? It had stemmed from there. As my fascination with happiness grew, I was curious about what would happen to a human being, living in a modern world, if you stripped them of pillars that we believe *stabilize* us: routine, social validation, and possessions, for instance.

Even 'possessions' become so tightly tied to ourselves that we call them 'belongings'. Because we hold a lot of 'must haves' in our head—we *must* have a home, we *must* have routine, we *must* be a part of a community, we *must* be surrounded by support, and the list goes on—I was curious about how many of them were as definitive as the way we state them.

This exercise was not a measure of hardship, as I was financially able to stop at any given time. I was fascinated by the spaces we often label as impossible: the 'I could never do that' space, the 'I could never live without . . .' space.

I was curious about what goes on inside us when we venture there, and society's response when we choose to live differently.

While the first week was easy, the remainder of the first month was hard. Before all this, I had never slept well on business trips, mainly because I have an irrational fear of ghosts so I sleep with *all* the lights on—including the bathroom light. However, at least business trips would come to an end after a week or two, so the build-up of poor sleep never went on for too long before I was back in *my own* bed, at *my own* home.

But this was not another business trip. As two weeks became three, four and onwards, the sense of homesickness grew stronger. I told myself, 'You can stop anytime, but let's just try and hold out for two months'.

In the beginning, I spoke little about my new way of life. As the weeks went by, I spent more time observing myself and how I was feeling. At first, I was spending more time on life admin than ever before, which was surprising, considering how little possessions I had. I had to ensure that all my bills and bank statements would be accessible online—anything sent to my physical mailbox would come with a phone notification. I had to check if I had any credit card renewals or important memberships that I needed to be prompt in retrieving. Essentially, a surge of things I never had to think about.

My first learning was that the world is not built for nomads. Certain banking documents *had to* be physically posted to you. I couldn't sign up for gym memberships or even go on free trials in some countries because I didn't have a physical address in that location. Sometimes, when the address was not required, the hiccup was that I didn't have a local mobile number. I couldn't tie my foreign bank account to WeChat pay in China or PromptPay in Thailand, and my ATM card let me withdraw cash only in some countries.

I never noticed these things when I travelled for work because I would usually stay at a hotel that was walking distance from the office. I'd have a packed schedule with work events, so rarely did I need more than the little bit of cash I exchanged at the airport. The hotel had a gym, and my experience of the country would comprise of the staple sequence of hotel > work > hotel > airport.

While I'm sure some hurdles I encountered may have been associated with user error, it was still glaringly obvious that the choice architecture of our societies conditions us to stay in one fixed place.

The nomadic norm of our ancestors is long gone, and my attempt at emulating some of that revealed the nudges designed to keep us in fixed locations. From the expectation of a Monday to Friday, 9 a.m. to 5 p.m. lifestyle, to the burden cycle of consumerism and debt, the system sucks you in, rewards conformity, and penalizes deviation. Like the Nokia 3310 game of snake, the system has set rules about where you can venture and where you can't. The longer you play it, the less room there is for you to move freely. And, before you know it, you've trapped yourself in an ever-narrowing circle of no escape—or so we lead ourselves to believe.

The more pushback I felt from the world, the more I was determined to keep at it.

Then, there was the clothing situation.

Black. Lots of black! In fact, I love bright colours, and yellow is my favourite. But black seemed to be the best choice when you only had twelve items of clothing that needed to cover every occasion. They're easy to match, are difficult to tell when dirty, and can pass off as both morning and evening outfits. Outfit situation at work was the easiest: same black top for three day a week, paired with either the work skirt or pants. A couple of different tops made up for the other two days. Done!

The fun part was twisting my brain to find ways to stretch the same items of clothing for weddings, out-out nights, and changing seasons. It wasn't just about moving from country-to-country, but also place-to-place within the same country. People would ask me to housesit while they were on holidays. This would usually be my longer stays, generally a week or two—during which I'd have the time to plan where to stay next—it might be on the same street, or a five-hour flight away.

Depending on my location of stay, I also had to figure out where I could wash my clothes. If I was at someone's house, it was easy—they would have a washing machine. But if I was at a hotel, doing laundry there could cost an exorbitant amount, so I'd have to find an alternative. Perhaps, I had a friend's place nearby where I could borrow their washing machine, or maybe I'd have to plan my next stop at an Airbnb. I also learned that you could negotiate terms with hoteliers if you stayed in chains frequently. Some offered up to three items of dry cleaning a day. It sounds tedious and overwhelming, but I loved it. It was like figuring out puzzles without an instructions sheet—there was no fixed image at the end of what my pieced-together puzzle had to look like. It forced me to be creative, and exercising it was fun!

It also put a fresh lens on how I felt about change: *Oh, we don't know what's going to happen in the next quarter?* That's fine. I don't even know where I'm going to be living next week!

Changes didn't feel daunting anymore, but instead, like the natural unfolding of life's surprises. This also meant I noticed how much energy people channelled into guessing, worrying, and talking about change. Usually, we address the symptom. For instance, we ask 'How are you feeling about this change?' then spend hours talking about whether we agree or disagree with the change in question, our discomforts and how do we ease them. We do this time and time again with every change that happens, instead of addressing the root cause, which is our relationship with change itself—our level of acceptance of life's impermanence. Instead of asking the question, 'How do you feel about *this* or *that* change?' focusing on a situation outside of us, we could instead be exploring, 'What is our relationship with change as a construct?', pivoting the attention inwards. If we can understand ourselves at this deeper level, then the importance of conversations about *this* or *that* change pales in comparison.

Then, there were the endless conversations about what the next change might be: situations where it was out of everyone's control and no one actually had an answer. Yet, there were waves of anxiety while everyone sought for certainty in an inherently uncertain climate.

'Live on the surface of life,' my meditation teacher once told me. If there is a situation, he meant, where you would never have the answer, let it be and move on. For example, if you receive a last-minute meeting cancellation, your mind starts going wild. 'How dare they do that to me? Do they not respect my time?' you might think. 'I bet they prioritized some other meetings over mine, which they would definitely have had more notice for, anyway. They should've said something. Maybe they are trying to convey their disapproval because of what happened in the last meeting. If we will never know the truth, then take the facts on surface level—we had a meeting, now it is canceled—then move on . . .'

Such thoughts go on and on.

Because my life now worked on five-to-ten-day phases—meaning I would change locations every five to ten days—it became necessary for me to take life as it comes. I couldn't commit to things until last minute, because I didn't know where I would be. This forced me to stay present because even the near future became unknown. I began to realize how much time we wasted discussing topics we'll never have the answers for: 'When will they announce the new CEO?', 'Why certain decisions were made?', 'What people might be thinking, or what it would have been like if . . .'

We are physically present, but mentally absent.

Aside from laundry and location, there was also the culling.

No more manicures and pedicures, since I was never somewhere long enough to be able to go back to the same salon. One weekend, at the beginning of my nomad journey, I spent an entire afternoon trying to find a nail salon to fix a chipped nail from a manicure I got in another country the week before. After that, I decided I would just stop doing them altogether.

As for hair, I started trying out the $10 haircuts boys go to, wherever was quick and didn't require me to make a booking. I must say, I was converted. No one could tell the difference between a $10 and $100 haircut. And, of course, I've never paid more than that since. In fact, my hairbrush broke halfway through the second month, so I decided to live without that too. I mean, fingers can operate like a hairbrush, and it freed up an extra bit of space in my suitcase! After all, when there's only one bag for all your stuff, every bit of space counts.

As time passed, I found myself opting to replace fewer and fewer items when they ran out. Shampoo and conditioner are plentiful pretty much everywhere, so there was really no need to be carrying my own. Hair gets dirty in a few days anyway, so whether it's a great shampoo or not, the effects only last a day or two.

My creativity also kicked in when I realized how many things could be substituted. Dab a bit of lipstick on your cheeks and it doubles up as blush, lip balm can also be a great face moisturiser, body and face wash are much the muchness, and a $6 tote from Cotton On is fitting for all occasions. Soon, this became a game I played with myself, where I would figure out how minimally I could possibly live. I felt excited when I ran out of something, as it gave me the opportunity to gauge if it could be substituted.

Travelling and packing meant very different things to me. I wasn't 'travelling' anymore; I was just living. And there was nothing to pack, because everything I had was right there. Once I got into the swing of things, my mind began to feel more and more spacious.

Aside from planning my next location, there wasn't much else I needed to consider on a daily basis. No more scrolling online for shopping, because there was nothing to shop for. I knew when I needed to buy something, because I would run out of it.

One out, one in. There was no physical space in my suitcase to consider buying anything else.

Then, suddenly, like the algorithm of the Backward Bike, it was as if a switch flicked, without me even realizing. I turned down the voices of the world and drew closer to Life. It was like walking up to the little five-year-old me in the playground, the girl who made up games for herself and sang songs nobody else could understand. In some strange way, it was like she helped me remember who I was, and who I could still be. I honestly don't remember the moment it happened, but something fundamentally shifted in me. From then on, the only thing that mattered to me was how alive I felt in people's presence. Soon, I developed a deep fascination of people's stories: what brought richness to their life, what inspired them, what hurt them, what wisdom have they discovered. On the other hand, what people were buying, what music did they listen to, what latest gadgets were released—all of that edged away into the distant.

All I knew was my interest in people had spiked. I loved everyday conversations. It was like I was that little girl during story time at school, listening intently with amazement at how incredible each of our lives are. Even when people were angry or lashing out, I would turn curious: *I wonder why they are acting like that? I wonder what unattended parts of them are needing to heal? How can I bring love into this space?*

In Buddhism, there is a type of meditation called *tonglen*, where you imagine you are breathing in the pain and frustration of those around you in the form of thick black smoke. As you take it in yourself, you convert it to light, exhaling it back to them in the form of love and blessings.

It became one of my favourite practices, especially with strangers. Soon, I found myself doing it whenever I was in a public place and had time to settle in. Some people feel uncomfortable with the idea of absorbing the pain from people around you, and many practices envision the opposite, soaking in light and love for yourself. While both are powerful visualizations, I particularly liked tonglen, as it meant I was also cultivating my own happiness by giving away love and blessings.

My teacher explained it to me through the principles of karma: What you give, you gain; what you take, you lose. So, by giving love, you gain love in return; and by taking in pain, you lose your own. Whenever I was on a crowded bus with everyone looking down on their phones, I would start my practice of giving away invisible gifts. Mostly, it was the light of love and blessings; other times, it would be personalized gifts: sending a flower, a hug, or a word of encouragement. Every time I did this, I finished feeling lighter, brighter, and more connected to our collective aliveness—Life.

Since the need for online shopping or endless doom scrolling didn't exist anymore, my phone, ironically, became the thing I used only for communication. I deleted unnecessary apps, making it a bare telephone rather than a supposed gateway to the world.

This meant my mind stayed where my body was. For example, if I was on the metro, I would be watching all the people with their heads down, on their phones, rather than being absorbed into my own phone. This also meant looking into the faces of those sitting opposite me and, if they happened to look up, I'd smile, even if they didn't reciprocate.

Once in a while, I would catch the awkward glance of someone, who wondered why I was making eye contact. A funny instance involved someone being unable to discern whether I was being a creep or friendly, and them offering an uncomfortable smile in return!

I would jump on random buses and get off whenever I felt like, in order to admire anything that had caught my attention. If I was curious about what someone was doing, I'd go up to them and ask. If I saw someone swaggy, I'd share the compliment with them. I'd greet the bus driver when I got on, then shouting, 'Thank you very much!' from the back of the bus as I got off at my stop. It was a strange way of what I would describe as 'being in the world'.

Things became simple.

I recall having breakfast with a friend on a Saturday morning. About an hour in, she told me she had to leave early, because she had ordered a piece of furniture that ended up being faulty. Upon returning it, the replaced item too turned out to be damaged. So, she spent an extra two hours contacting customer service, and had to go all the way to the factory to select a new one.

I remember feeling the intensity of her frustration as she told her story. But I also remember thinking: *Wow, that's a lot of time spent on a chair.*

I didn't own furniture anymore, hence I struggled to comprehend how one little *thing* could create so much commotion. After my friend left, I felt even less enamoured by *stuff.*

After lunch, while my friend was frantically sorting out the chair situation, I cruised slowly back to my parent's place, walked around the garden, felt the sun on my skin, and gentle breeze brush over my face. Breathing in the crisp morning air, I noticed a small yellow flower growing up through the cracks between the driveway tiles. I bent down to take a look, and remembered how amazed I was seeing its incredible life force growing against all odds!

It was like reverting to a version 2.0 of myself, while everyone was chasing version 12.0. It was an interesting feeling, as if I was regressing and advancing at the same time, because I was happier—*so* much happier. There was no part of me that wanted to rejoin the crowd I had separated from. I still loved interacting with people, but in a different way. It was like I was living in another dimension of life. While I was the only one who seemed to be in such a space, I felt more connected to everything and everyone, more than ever. It was a belonging to myself that allowed me to offer more love to the world, as I was no longer concerned about how *I* looked, what *I* needed, and what *I* was missing.

One day, someone asked how this 'suitcase living' lifestyle had been going. I felt stumped for a second . . . because I had completely forgotten that I was a nomad! Once my mind had clicked into the algorithm of such a way of living, it no longer felt strenuous or abnormal. And, before I knew it, I had already been over a year into it.

People usually have a long list of questions, which I answer, then politely nod when they reply with, 'I could never do what you do,' or 'I wish I could do what you do, but I can't,' or 'I want to do that, but I've missed my window'. However, the truth is, we all can. Some people have greater logistical hurdles than others, such as those with responsibilities that extend beyond themselves. But for the most part, it's a very doable thing. What really holds people back is not the logistics, it's the fear of shaking up everything they've worked to put in place. We lock ourselves in a golden cage, forgetting the strength of our wings and the thrill of the open air. Maybe you haven't *needed* to, or *wanted* to, but there is no question about your capability.

When we think back to challenges our parents, grandparents, or people we know faced, we are often shocked by how they managed to survive in the conditions they did. My friend's mother, who was in Cambodia during the Khmer Rouge regime, told me how, in a matter of days, she went from being a dainty city girl to working the fields with leeches on her legs, having to kill chicken for food with her bare hands. She'd never thought of doing this in her life, and while it was traumatizing, it was an experience that revealed how resilient she could be. A few years later, she fell down the escalators at a shopping mall. When my friend ran down to help her, he saw her sitting there, leg gushing with blood, but with a big bright smile on her face. 'It's nothing, all good,' she said. 'Let's get me to the hospital and they'll fix me right up.'

He stood there in shock. Though he knew she had gone through a lot growing up, he struggled to understand how she was so at ease—even in a situation as painful as that.

Their stories, like many others', speaks to our innate resilience—the one we deny ourselves as we wander within our realm of comfort. While it is not to say we should put ourselves in the way of harm to experience trauma, it is an invitation to challenge our own thinking when we say, 'I can't'. Each time we say this, we close off possibilities. We wilfully shrink our world, making us forget that 'I can't' is more often a choice than an absolute.

So, next time you catch yourself saying, 'I can't', rephrase and say, 'I choose not to,' instead. By doing this, we honour our capability. This change in language empowers you as the chooser of your life, rather than the victim—barred from the places we 'can't' go to.

Remember: 'I choose not to,' also keeps the door open for a different choice, on another day. Maybe one day, that 'I choose not to', will turn into 'I choose to try,' and maybe by trying, you might just do it!

While recording a podcast, my co-host asked me if it was okay to share with someone his experience with me. 'Sure,' I replied, not knowing what he was referring to. He began to divulge. 'I went for coffee with Judy, and it was her turn to pay. However, when she approached the counter, instead of pulling out her wallet she pulled out one of those plastic zip lock bags you use to put sandwiches in,' he said. 'That was her wallet! Credit card and all! My mind was blown. This girl really does not give a damn!'

I laughed, not having realized it was shocking to him. Now, when I think back, its unusualness had never even crossed my mind. I suppose most of us believe that money *must* be kept in a wallet, but with me trying to live as minimally as possible, I had chosen a 'simpler' alternative. While that small action had lightened my load, it also inspired someone to see possibility in a place they previously did not.

What I hadn't expected was how the nomadic experience changed my interactions with people. What I thought would distance me from people became, very quickly, the shortcut to getting closer to them instead. Now, I no longer believe that rapport and connection take time, because it all depends on where you start. If your starting point is, 'This is what I do, and this is all that I have accomplished,' of course, it is going to take time, as you are busy flashing your armour at people, rather than allowing them to connect with your humanness.

But if your starting point is, 'I'm using my life as a social experiment, so I gave away 90 per cent of my belongings and I'm currently living out of a suitcase,' then your relationship with that person starts in a completely different place, a realm of curiosity exploration.

The rote learned ways of building rapport—introduce what you do, your elevator pitch, and talk about your shiny accolades—shows off some badges, but reveals nothing about who you are.

I was once sitting next to an older gentleman at dinner. *Oo! I bet he has lots of exciting stories*, I thought to myself. I smiled, and before I could say a single word, he launched into a half-an-hour monologue about how everyone in his family has a PhD. His kids, his grandkids, his distant cousins . . . and when it finally seemed like I could ask a question, he proceeded to tell me about where they work and how important they are. It was one of the most draining conversations of my life, and all I did was sit there! After his monologue, I left, knowing absolutely nothing about him.

This unconscious reiteration attaches our identities and self-worth to our jobs, companies, families, and communities. Therefore, it makes sense that people say rapport building takes time, because we need to break through shields of armour before we touch anything real.

If you're thinking, 'But I'm boring, and there is nothing outstanding about who I am', think again. We see what we give energy to, and if we've been so accustomed to belonging to our badges, then it's natural for this shift to feel difficult.

Here is a tip: talk about what you believe in, not what you do. The former is infinitely richer than a standard job title or a role you play in this world. What you believe in sparks aliveness in both you and the person you're with. It also sends you an unconscious message that your realness is more valuable than your badges. Try it, and notice the difference when you start connecting with people on this level: how you feel, how they respond. We can chart a new path, and when we do, it's not just for ourselves but for everyone else who you share the journey with. In taking ourselves beyond the norm, we offer those around us a refreshing splash of new energy. It is absolutely possible, but it must start with you.

What if they start the conversation though, and ask me the standard rapport building questions? When people ask me what I do, I reply with, 'I do my best'. It would usually be returned with a laugh or sheepish smile, which is the perfect segway into a far more enriching conversation. 'When does life feel most alive for you?' I would ask, or perhaps, 'Who is someone who changed your life, but doesn't know it?' What ensues from there is far richer and fruitful than an exchanging of job titles. Even as people try to steer you back to the beaten track, you can always steer your way out.

When you interrupt the flow of someone's habitual patterns, you throw them into a momentary state of confusion. This is the point where mentalists or hypnotists move in with a direct suggestion, because it is when we are most susceptible. Another way of seeing this is when you ask an out-of-the-ordinary question, you create space, an environment that is unknown, where there are no rehearsed responses or predefined rules of how to continue. In this space, you allow yourself and others to extend beyond the habitual in co-creating something new, something *alive*.

I was once at a conference, where, over lunch, I sat around a table of leaders doing the usual job title exchange. Instead of following suit, I threw out a question to the table: What is your message to the world?

Followed by a long silence, one person said. 'Oh, wow. How do I answer this? I've never been asked this before.' That sharing of silent reflection buzzed with aliveness. We spent the next hour exchanging stories from our lives that moved us, and the difference we wanted to create in this world.

'I want my child to grow up in a happier world,' said one lady. 'I want people to see that even their most mundane lives have meaning,' said the gentleman across from me. 'Can I read you all a poem?' another asked.

'Of course!' we replied. And suddenly, our conference table felt more like a circle around a camp fire, as we listened to her poem about remembering what truly matters in life. At the end of the hour, we all agreed that it was an unexpected detour that had led to an incredibly fulfilling experience, and it all happened because of one powerful question.

The more I broke away from the habitual patterns of interaction, the more I realized how assumptions of the world go scarily unchallenged. We box ourselves in our heads, seeing ourselves as helpless to the forces of our environment when we have every power to recreate a new reality. If there was a way *into* the box, then there definitely is a way out. We disconnect from our aliveness, develop a sea of shallow relationships, then blame the world for being transactional. All this, while never accepting responsibility that we have contributed to it.

If we want to breakthrough the confines of our environment, we can start by taking ownership of our happiness. Become cognizant of the conditioning that got us into the box, listen for the words that trapped us there, and live intentionally. Distance allows for perspective, and non-attached belonging lets us return to our creativity and imagination. 'Every whisper of a dream can become a roaring reality,' can be a message to us from our five-year-old-selves.

One of the most difficult things I found was reassuring people who loved and cared for me. The gentle questions of, 'Are you *sure* you're okay?' or the upfront, in-your-face, 'What the hell are you doing with your life?'

Either way, living differently comes with more concern than praise—especially with parents, many of us live to make them proud, and the thought of disappointing them is often too painful to fathom. Their expectations of us often come from believing they know what's best: good education, friends, career, and eventually, marry into a good family. Each loving wish carries with it an expectation, and each expectation the weight of responsibility to live up to them. The honour of responsibility drowns out our curiosity to explore, and we resort to disappointing ourselves and justifying it as duty.

While my choice to live nomadically troubled my friends and family, my discovery was worth every conversation of repeatedly assuring everyone that I was okay. What kept me steady was the knowing that irrespective of how or what I did, they wanted me to be happy, and their concern came from fear that I might be running away from something I didn't dare face. I could understand why they thought so, and they urged me to rejoin the crowd, for it was predictable and 'safe'. When we deviate from the crowd, the assumption is that something is wrong, but maybe it's the very opposite, something is *really* right.

Those who listen to my story in admiration got me wondering: What did they see in my experience, and why did they want that for themselves? How come more people didn't do this when the timing may have worked? What other things do we let pass us by, only to look back later in life and feel like we missed the train? What does 'the train' look like, and when do we know that our train has arrived? What was the train you missed? What train is at your station now, that if you don't awaken to, will become a missed train too?

I describe this experience like breaking through a balloon. While you're inside it, your brain rewards you for conforming, and you feel at ease. However, when you start moving towards the edges of the balloon, tension builds. The voices of disagreement beckon you to turn around. Sometimes, they're loud with anger; other times, they are silent with disappointment. If you are curious enough about what's out there, and if you believe there's something greater than the balloon we are in, keep going. The intensity of pressure from people will increase, but at some point, you will breakthrough—pop!

And just like that, you'll switch into a new algorithm, and you begin living in a whole new world.

It may just be an even bigger balloon, and perhaps, at some point, you want to test its limits too. This is exactly how we grow, feeling the discomfort and moving through it, instead of bouncing back the moment you feel tension. Let the discomfort ignite curiosity and suffering signal opportunity to learn something new. All things shall pass, including the disapproving voices. At some point, people give up, because you're not the main character of their life, they are. When people see that the unknown you have ventured into is your heart's calling, that you are happy, and it's not as catastrophic as they originally dramatized in their minds, they move on. Some will rejoice seeing you happy, others might sit silently in jealousy. Either way, it reveals more about them than anything you've done.

I lived for over two years out of a suitcase, and those were some of the best years of my life.

REFLECTING

A corporate leader, minimalist, and nomad, I gave away 90 per cent of my possessions and navigated life from a suitcase. While this journey lacked the foundations most seek in life – stability, routine, and material comforts, it revealed a dimension of life that lies beneath the surface of our day-to-day interactions.

While we play out life in habitual ways, with rote learned scripts about who we are and what we do, we can break that pattern with a provoking question, creating space for people to set down their armour, and instead, bring forth their raw, unfiltered humanity.

Ponder

- Which parts of my identity feel most resistant to change, and what might that resistance reveal about my deeper fears or desires?
- How would you live differently if you trusted that you could navigate discomfort and uncertainty?
- What is cool about 'weird'? How can you honour the weird in you?

Be Your Own Self Coach

Practice introducing yourself without using a badge that ties your identity to a person or place. For example, 'I am a father,' is tied to your role in the family, or 'I am an accountant,' is tied to your role in an organization. Take some time to consider what you are without these badges, and what impact having them has on the way you lead your life.

Beyonding

Bronnie Ware worked in palliative care. Her patients were those who only had a few weeks left to live, and she cared for them in their last days. When she asked them whether they had regrets or would do anything differently, the most common regret was, 'I wish I'd had the courage to life a life true to myself, not the life others expected of me.'

Refer to the picture below and channel your ninety-year-old self in the reflection.

As you look at the future you, the version of you that continued down the trajectory you are on now, what do they want you to know? What do they know you need to hear now?

Chapter 8

CREATING SPACE

Beyond belonging is somewhere you get to by choosing your inner knowing over and over. Your choice to follow your voice within, which only you can hear, may face ridicule, disapproval, and disappointment—emotions that tug at our heartstrings.

Firstly, practice becoming the observer of your life. Imagine you are looking down at yourself from a bird's eye view, noticing what you see when you're no longer the subjective experiencer. Secondly, give yourself the opportunity to choose yourself. What might one small step in choosing yourself look like? Thirdly, share your journey with others., Your bravery in creating space for yourself will ignite the flame for others who have also toyed with the idea of breaking free. Remember: Our five-year-old selves are always with us, waiting for us to remember the version of us who dared to dream, who knew were destined for the extraordinary.

When did you last give yourself the permission to decide for yourself? What is your definition of a life well-lived? If someone was reading your eulogy at your funeral, what story would they tell about your life?

To create space means to take a powerful pause when people tell you to go-go-go, to feel the guilt of falling short of people's expectations, but choosing yourself anyway. To wake up to the path right for us, we need space, perspective, and self-compassion. Our full power doesn't come from following the maps written by others.

Alice works at a hospice. Surrounded by death and dying, her work carries a heavy emotional weight. Her autistic son has also been unwell for the last few years, and recently, she learned that her daughter is also struggling at school. Her father-in-law passed away a few months ago, and she is supporting her husband as he grieves.

She is far beyond the pleasantries. When asked how she's doing, her response, albeit with a warm smile, is this: 'Not great, actually,' she says. 'Not good at all.'

When asked what could be of help to her, her reply is clear. 'Self-compassion and space,' she says. 'Having kids is like taking your heart, ripping it out of your chest, and having it walk around outside of you—never knowing what will happen next.' One realizes that parenting will never end, she explains, and that we will always care for our children—even when they aren't physically dependent on you.

'Going to work helps me a lot,' she says, 'I needed a degree of autonomy, where I could step out of my role as a mom, as a wife, and literally don a new set of clothes and be me.'

While many think her job is emotionally burdensome, for her, it's a place of self-care and self-compassion. 'It reminds me that I am also a human being, that I am also dying, and that puts things into perspective. When your kids are young, they need you. You are literally joined at the hip, and it's as if your identity merges with theirs. But as they get older, it's not healthy for either of us.'

Creating separation is key, Alice feels. 'We have to be kind and nurture ourselves, before we can be fully there for others.' For as long as we attach our identity to others, we impose pressures and expectations that limit their ability to be themselves.

She strongly disagrees with the statement, 'I just want you to be happy,' stressing that she would never say it to anyone, particularly her children. 'How can someone be happy on demand?' she asks. 'If their life's purpose is to be happy for my sake, it's too big a bind!'

Instead, she has a different approach. 'I just want them to be *them*, while I can be *me*,' she says. 'It gives us freedom to be happy—and not.' In essence, she believes we can allow each other to show up as ourselves, free from the coercion of expectation. When we have the space to show up as who we are, we offer other people the opportunity to see us for who we are. It is within this space of authenticity that true connection is built. I need not belong to you; you need not belong to me, and in this non-attached state, we are able to simply *be*.

Non-attachment does not mean indifference. The latter is disinterest or not caring, whereas the former is the practice of letting go. Non-attached belonging fosters compassion, allowing us to engage with the world, without being ensnared by it.

'I have had to change my idea of what a good life is,' says Alice, who loves travelling and learning new things. 'Those are my aspirations. But my son has told me he really doesn't enjoy it. He likes to be in a room with his friends, playing games, where they move around small pieces of who-knows-what on a board. It is the most boring, life-draining thing. But he lights up playing it!'

Though Alice will live to her aspirations, she is also learning to love her son in his way, allowing him space to move towards his own definition of a good life, because at the end of the day, only he is responsible for his own happiness.

'We can either learn from other people's experiences and let it expand us, or we can shun it for being different to ours and makes ourselves smaller,' she says.

Space creates the perspective that brings us choice. When we are buried in cultural conditioning, it is difficult to see the system we are in. We spend more time complaining about the system than doing something about it.

The behaviours and decisions we make each day are guided by invisible forces, and we spend a large chunk of our lives unconscious, moving through the motions with little question or choice for ourselves. However, if we can create space consciously, we can wake up to our patterns, giving ourselves a chance to reshape our reality.

We can create physical space, venturing beyond our current routines to check out a new place by ourselves. We can also create emotional space by bravely delving into our inner world, confronting the parts we armour up—the grief, the anger, the longing—and letting it speak without censoring.

We can also create space by interacting with our environment mindfully. Closing your eyes and listening for the furthest thing you can hear for ten seconds, then listening for the closest thing you can hear for ten seconds. Feeling the texture of the page with your fingertips, journaling, or spending time in nature can all help us create space between our inner and outer worlds.

Space is also about pausing. Each time you notice yourself in an unresourceful state, pause. Feeling what you feel, hearing what you hear, seeing what you see. Not responding, just pausing to fully experience what's happening. Do it for as long as it takes for that urge to subside, and if it returns, pause some more. The more you do it, the more you deplete the habit of go-go-go. Take yourself for a walk, take a path you have never walked before, and let the freshness of the new space inspire you. Invite an outlier into your life, listen to their story with both your ears and your heart, allow their difference to take you into another reality.

By interrupting our patterns with space, we take the brave leap into compassionate inquiry. I say 'compassionate', because our negativity bias can easily spiral down a storyline of self-blame. So, by such an inquiry, I mean to question with curiosity and self-love, knowing that you did the best you could with the resources you had.

Ask yourself: What stories am I telling myself? What is my body trying to tell me? What part of me have I neglected? This process of close examination can feel frighteningly insecure for it reveals to us the unsettling aspects of our lives we attempt to avoid.

Each time you feel the tension, give it breath. Do it in the same way you breathe into a tight muscle. Watch as your breath travels to that part of tension and softens it, transforming it into gentle unfolding awareness.

There you go.

Feel the message of what that awareness shows you. It may feel groundless, because creating space is the opposite of jumping from one thing to another, it is the emptiness between ideologies. It is the unknown between the two poles of certainty, and while a sense of surety feels fixed and secure, it's in the space of in-between that wisdom is found. Creating space is about renegotiating our relationship with the messiness of who we are.

If doing it on your own feels too overwhelming, create space with the support of a professional. A coach can help you create space through powerful questions, inciting exploration in areas of yourself you have yet to consider. A therapist helps in addressing emotional or psychological needs, creating space for you to heal past trauma or conditions that hold you back. A mentor is a partnership with someone further down the line than you, offering wisdom and guidance based on their experience. While beyond belonging is ultimately about tuning into your own voice, a mentor can also be your first port of call in helping you breakthrough fixed ideologies. They can be your outlier, helping you identify alternatives that you have yet to consider.

Mentoring SG, a national movement in Singapore recognizes the need to broaden our perspectives of success.[27] For them, it's critical that people gain perspectives beyond their immediate circle of family and friends.

While their work currently focuses on the youth, it highlights the power of mentorship in helping people step beyond their mental bubble, with 86 per cent of mentees finding the experience beneficial.

In an insightful study, titled 'State of Youth Mentoring in Singapore', mentoring was most sought-after during times of transition, a momentary pause between life stages where we can reevaluate and reorient.[28] It 'open[s] your eyes to possibilities,' said one mentee, describing what it was like to engage with someone outside their social network. However, when it came to resilience in carrying out change, some found that mentoring supported it, while others felt it was a journey to be walked alone. 'Resilience is something within yourself,' said another mentee. 'It's not something people can influence you [to have]', it is 'still up to you'. So, while mentors can spark insight, it is still up to us to do the work.

Mentee-mentor compatibility was a critical factor impacting engagement. It was important for them to be matched with someone they could build rapport with, felt they could trust and believed in them: a safe space for personal exploration. As expected, if the mentor and mentee possessed certain similarities, 'the more suitable mentees perceived their mentors to be'. Like the smelly T-shirt study, our judgement skews towards favourable when we feel like there is shared commonality.

However, they also uncovered an interesting anomaly. 'While the suitability of values and beliefs, personality, life challenges, and career experiences positively influences mentee-mentor rapport', religion negatively influences it.

This means that there was lower rapport between mentors who shared the same religion as their mentees. While the reasoning behind this remains inconclusive, and further research is recommended, it raises a fascinating question: Could certain aspects of shared identity inadvertently reinforce inherited expectations, making it harder for mentees to have space in exploring their own unique path?

Perhaps for some of the youth in this study, the framework of religion may feel more restrictive than welcoming. Since our initial experiences with religion are often shaped by the traditions and teachings passed down from our parents, we often face pressure to follow doctrines and dogmas in early stages of our life. It is only later, through space—breaking free from our parents' expectations of how religion should be followed—that we arrive at our own relationship with the divine.

Creating space is not an act of rebellion; it is an opportunity to course correct. Our life offers liminal phases for us to pause and reevaluate. However, what if creating space became a conscious part of our daily lives: like Alice, making a conscious effort to create space for herself, even when her family clings to her for support, or like some mentees who sought out mentors even when they weren't in transitional periods? Our inner wisdom is always with us, and we need not wait for times of struggle and despair before we tap into it.

We are conditioned for tunnel vision: we go, we go, and we go. We work ourselves to burnout, mindlessly following instructions, cementing our belonging in the golden cage of 'it's just life'. To find meaning, we must wake up. When we pause to question, to engage in compassionate inquiry, we may come to notice that the door to the cage was always open. We might stretch our wings and take flight, or we might still choose to stay. But *choosing* to stay is different from believing in the illusion that there is no cage, or seeing the cage but feeling like there is no escape. A choice to stay is also a form of freedom.

'Birds born in a cage think flying is an illness'
—Alejandro Jodorowsky

REFLECTING

Stepping back from the places or people we've held onto with all our heart can feel like ripping ourselves apart. The pain is real and raw. But here, we may discover a new way of being. This unfamiliar freedom is often met with misunderstanding. People judge, label, and try to reel us back in, wanting us to fit in. Yet, the greatest gift to this world is to honour our truth so we can be the fullest expression of ourselves.

Each step into the unknown offers a chance to rediscover the parts of ourselves we had buried to belong. Returning to ourselves, with childlike wonder, we can set our own rules, dare to be curious, dream and redefine life on our own terms. Finding authenticity, even when it feels uncomfortable.

Ponder

- In what ways do I define myself by my relationships?
- What happens when those relationships change?
- When have I allowed for physical, emotional, or mental space in my life?
- What holds me back from creating more space?

Be Your Own Self Coach

Draw three concentric circles, labelling them as 'Outer', 'Middle' and 'Inner'. Within each layer, write down your responses to the below:

The Outer You

Write down all the roles you hold e.g. daughter, leader, friend etc. Write down how each role defines your sense of self, what expectations there are of both you and others. If you were to let go of this role, even just temporarily, how would that feel?

The Middle You

List five values that feel core to who you are—for example, curiosity, freedom, and creativity etc. How much space does this value currently hold in your life? In what areas are you living true to this value? Where are you compromising?

The Inner You

If you were completely free from expectations or judgement, what thoughts, behaviours, and habits would you have? What small step can you take to invite this feeling of freedom more?

Beyonding

Find a recent photo of yourself, and do this exercise while looking at that photo.

Step 1: Write a full-page description of yourself, starting each sentence with:

- This is someone who . . .
- This is someone who . . .
- This is someone who . . .
- This is someone who . . .
- This is someone who . . .
- This is someone who . . .
- This is someone who . . .
- This is someone who . . .
- This is someone who . . .
- This is someone who . . .
- This is someone who . . .
- This is someone who . . .
- This is someone who . . .
- This is someone who . . .
- This is someone who . . .
- This is someone who . . .
- This is someone who . . .
- This is someone who . . .
- This is someone who . . .
- This is someone who . . .

Step 2: Take a black marker and begin crossing out everything that doesn't feel truly you. Anything that feels like it was imposed on you, anything that was out of tradition or expectation, rather than your own choosing. Traits or roles you've outgrown, judgements, labels or 'shoulds'. Be honest and be bold. You're not editing—you're censoring the false self. The goal is to see what's left when the noise is gone.

Step 3: Now, read what remains, the lines that survived. What surprised you about what you censored out? What patterns did you notice? How can you make more space for you to return to your true self?

I will gift myself space by...

Chapter 9

REMEMBERING YOU

Remember that five-year-old you.

In a memory so distant, we can barely recall the time when we moved with the wind and danced to the beat in our hearts—when we laughed and cried whenever we wanted, and ran around naked with no concept of shame. A time when we didn't seek for permission to be ourselves, where the world was simply a playground where we were joyful inhabitants. We sat on the floor and played with our toys for hours and nothing else mattered. Life was simple: eat, play, poop, sleep—in no particular order! Just whatever we felt like, whenever we felt like. Adults circled us, trying to figure out what we wanted, when in truth, we probably didn't know ourselves.

We were just *being.* Our life burned with aliveness: pure and untamed. We didn't carry the burdens of expectations, of *shoulds* and *should nots,* of comparison or judgements. We never sought for anyone to validate our worth; we were happily ourselves. We lived every experience as it came, like a bright new light bulb, shining with brilliant clarity.

Chapter 9.1 – Observing From Beyond

When we get caught up in the world, breakthrough demands courage.

As the subjective experiencer of our lives, our depth of immersion in roles creates the illusion of 'the only way'. Take, for instance, flying home to see your parents and feeling like 'the only way' is staying with them, even when living separately would give everyone a bit more breathing space; or being pressured to pursue a particular career because it is 'the only way' to succeed, even though academia was never your strength.

There comes a point when stepping back is not selfish, but critical. The lens of the objective observer is the necessary perspective for us to see what's really going on. When we pull away from deep attachments, we see clearer, giving ourselves the capacity to remember who we were before the world told us who we ought to be.

Lorna was your quintessential Christian. Growing up in the US, she attended church with her parents every Sunday. When she had a family of her own and moved to Beijing, weekly church and Bible study continued to be part and parcel of their lives.

'I was so caught up in it, and I was conditioned to say the words and walk the talk, but it never felt quite right,' she said. 'But it's hard to go against the grain, and I don't think that I could've just stepped out, because I wasn't brave enough to be judged by the entire religion.'

She also loves worship music. 'When I listen to worship music, I feel the holy spirit in me, and it's affirming. Maybe people in other religions feel it too, I don't know. I was just taught that anything outside of Christianity was bad, and therefore, I never got to experience otherwise.'

When she and her family moved to Hong Kong, something changed.

For the first time in her life, she was not attached to the church—the place she had always known. It almost felt like leaving an organization she would have otherwise been a part of her whole life. 'It shaped how I spoke, my psyche, and even how I felt,' so to suddenly be out of it felt scary. Now, physically removed, something profound began to happen.

There was unspoken permission to venture beyond the walls that once defined her, although she still walked cautiously with the weight of others' opinion on her shoulders. 'There were so many people from church who followed me on Instagram,' she said. Venturing beyond, she was in a space she hadn't realized she needed. And there, she began to see things differently.

No longer surrounded by the unspoken expectations, or the ever-present judgement, it felt like traveling to a new land: like standing on the edge of the ocean, realizing there was an entire world beyond her previous reality. 'There was a kind of magic in stepping sideways,' she said. 'Like walking through a door you didn't know existed: vast, mysterious, and full of possibilities'. She took up *chi gong*, learned about energy and breathwork, and connected to the intelligence of her body.

'Your body does not lie to you. We're just so wired up we never listen to it,' she said. On this journey, she began to realize how much she had been neglecting herself. 'I have a Type-A personality. I like to get involved in everything,' she exclaims. 'I love doing everything!'

She is a mother, wife, global leader, tennis league player, and the centre of many social circles. 'I was so busy doing everything that I forgot to give my body the most basic of nourishment: to breathe,' she said. 'I noticed that I was always holding my breath. I spoke a lot, and didn't inhale enough deep breaths into the belly. I was starving by body of breath—the very source of our life.'

On a breathwork retreat, she came to understand the root cause of many of her ailments..

Every conscious breath became an invitation to return to herself, worrying less about the voices of others, as she turned to her inner guide. 'It's right here,' she said, patting her chest. 'I can feel it'.

The more she listened to her body, the more it started reminding her of past stories, the unprocessed parts of her childhood she had tucked away in the shadows. She started to observe the situations where she felt imbalanced, the times she acted out of obligation than love, situations that did not nourish her, but she did it anyway.

She began to differentiate between 'outward' and 'inward' belonging. 'We're always looking outwards,' she said, 'looking for belonging outside of ourselves to define us'. And it was when she moved her attention inwards, that she found a deeper belonging, one she describes as aligning with the rhythm of her soul.

'I can still belong to places and people, but first I belong to myself,' she says now. 'Sometimes, the sense of belonging will confuse your journey. But before anything, we must be okay in our own centre. If someone comes along and contributes to it, it surely brightens us. If not, that's okay too—it doesn't affect our core. We are social animals, but our home and our belonging is our own to nurture. We shouldn't expect anyone else to do that for us.'

Now, every time she feels a sense of imbalance, instead of pushing it away, she slows down, observes, and feels. As much as she wants to continue launching forward, she pulls back, gives it breath, and observes.

She began to realize that the feeling she experienced in church—the sense of something larger than herself—wasn't confined to a single religion or belief system. 'I still feel the holy spirit,' she says. 'But now, it is also the universe, chi, and prana. I wouldn't have had that revelation if I hadn't stepped away.'

In another part of the world, Yvonne also felt the call of her inner wisdom.

Having married a good friend and started a dentistry business together, she thought they were starting to pursue a dream together until they had kids. Something nudged her to pay attention, but as the 'good Asian wife', she ignored it and told herself that she should continue the trajectory she had started. 'I lost who I was; I had forgotten what I really wanted,' she said.

Even though, as a kid, her father always encouraged her to explore and be bold, somewhere, somehow she lost her way. She slipped into a socialized mindset rather than one of self-authoring. Ironically, all of this reflection took place while she was writing a book. It dawned on her how miserable she was.

'Do I live in this world? Or do I live in my own?' she asked herself.

By then, it didn't take much to recognize that her marriage had not been serving her or her husband. The relationship, which was supposed to help them grow, had stagnated them, and they were always having to go along with the other.

As she began to tune into her inner voice, a whisper called her to 'a certain adventure'. And that was the beginning of a journey of ten years as she started to rebuild her confidence to step out again, on her own. She describes that period as a time when she was 'not honest with him, nor with my own self.'

When she finally felt strong enough to take on an opportunity in Qatar, she moved over with the kids. Her husband joined for a little while, but soon realized it was not for him, and so, he left. Now they were in a long-distance relationship.

'It gave me space to meditate on my situation, become more reflective, and see what I could actually achieve on my own.' This space marked the beginning of her journey home to herself.

Soon, with a heavy heart, she made the choice to end her marriage—a decision that was tough on the family then, and would be, difficult for years to come. 'We were meant to live happily ever after,' her kids told her, blaming her for not trying hard enough, and for breaking up the family.

One day, she received a note from her kids, aged fourteen and sixteen at the time, saying they would like her to leave them alone, no longer wishing to communicate with her.

In a moment of quiet despair, just after receiving the heartbreaking note from her children, fate intervened. As if guided by something greater, she bumped into her retired therapist in the warmth of a coffee shop, a quiet miracle amid the pain she was in.

After listening to the situation, the therapist asked, 'How do you feel about this?'

After some reflection, she said, 'You know, what? I love them so much for standing up for what they felt—for speaking up and not clamming up, which is what I've been doing for the last ten years of my marriage. So, secretly, I'm proud of them. I love them for who they are, but, of course, I don't appreciate this behaviour.'

'Show them then,' her therapist told her.

And so she did.

For three years, Yvonne wrote them letters with no response. 'You don't have to answer my letters, but I will continue to write to you as your mother,' she wrote. 'I love you; I love you no matter what.'

She never knew if her words reached them, or where the letters ended up. All she could hold onto was the love she carried for them, and that she would keep writing to them, even in their silence.

One day, she suddenly received a call from her son. When she picked up, he was bawling. 'Mom, I'm sorry I never opened the letters,' he said through his tears. It was clear that he only just understood how hard the journey had been for her. Thank you for standing up [for her decision]. It really taught me a lot about relationships,' he said, crying.

He had kept all the letters in his cupboard. One day, while cleaning it, he decided to read them. 'My kids grew up. They realized that Mom had to take a stand, just like they did. And soon, we became closer again. Sometimes, when you follow your heart, it means you have to make tough calls,' she said.

Yvonne, who describes herself as a wacky leader, an outlier who moves against the temptations of socialization, describes her process of choosing a life of self-sovereignty in the face of societal pressure. 'There is a soul or a spirit in us, designed to express our genius or talents,' she says. 'That's what we're born with, to contribute to the world.'

Each time she chose the voice in her heart over the opinions of the world, she drew closer to the self she had once walked away from. As she leaned into the hard work of observing her thoughts and feelings, the scattered parts of her began to return.

On the last day of a meditation retreat, as she sang along to Michael Jackson's 'You Are Not Alone', she felt the energy around her shift. There, in the fading light, shapes began to form, emerging like familiar figures stepping out of a dream. The imaginary friends she had sent away at the age of twelve had returned, standing before her, glowing in their full radiance. They were the parts of her she had left behind for adulthood. Each friend, each figure, representing a fragment of her soul that had been forgotten and hidden away. Now, they were back, knowing that she was ready to walk home with them to wholeness.

Her heart expanded, overflowing with a sense of reunion and completeness, understanding that she had never been broken, only separated. As she welcomed them home, she felt the warmth of her entire being now woven together in unity. With a deep breath, she smiled, knowing that she was never alone, and they would live in her heart forevermore.

We are all invited to come home to ourselves. To reunite with the parts we lost touch with along the way. We wear labels like badges of honour, growing accustomed to bearing its weight on our soul. However, every step we take beyond them is growth. Whether it is choosing your own beliefs about tradition, or resigning from a job for reasons only you understand, you owe it to yourself to stand for what you know in your heart but no one else can see: not for reward, recognition, or righteousness, but in honour of yourself.

You are the only person who is guaranteed to walk this life with you, and each time we place our belonging outside of us, we are distracted from the home within. Doctors will give you medication without asking about your lifestyle, psychologists will work with your mind without understanding your body, and everyone will give you directions on where to go—without ever knowing the compass in your heart.

It may feel isolating to walk the journey beyond belonging, but the way home inward is never walked alone.

REFLECTING

We naturally entangle ourselves in roles, environments and expectations that shape our identity without question. The well-intended gathering of people, be in religion, family, or any other setting, serve as a place of belonging and security.

However, when we step back from being the subjective experiencer and take on the perspective of an objective observer, we begin to see the confines and limitations of these places. Our intuition nudges us to go beyond, to reconnect with ourselves and trust our inner wisdom as we discover what is really meant for us, decided by us.

Ponder

- What roles and environments have shaped my identity, and do they still serve me?
- What beliefs do I hold that might not be my own?
- What aspects of myself have I abandoned or suppressed to 'fit in'?

Be Your Own Self Coach

It's difficult to capture the full picture when we're engrossed in it. Hence taking on a meta position, an elevated or detached perspective, helps us open our eyes. As you sit in your situation, imagine stepping outside of yourself to observe your experience from the perspective of an onlooker. What do you see from here?

Take this further by imaging you are high up in a helicopter, and now, you are viewing yourself down below, and all that is around you. What do you notice from here?

From this meta position, you are emotionally neutral as you are no longer yourself. You begin to see the dynamics at play, your biases and things around you that were blind to you before. What insights have you gained from this experience? How can you bring more power back for yourself?

Another way to do this is to seek the perspective of an outlier, someone who is an onlooker of your life, and holds beliefs that are starkly different to yours. This requires great commitment to openness in accepting their perspective, approaching it with curiosity rather than defensiveness.

Chapter 9.2 – Home

Even when we have lost awareness of who we once were, our unconscious remembers. The unconscious mind is an infinite storage unit, quietly absorbing and storing every experience. Take this moment as an example: reading this book. Your conscious mind is taking in the words, your unconscious is digging through your archives to connect the dots. It is also absorbing everything else: the moisture of the room, the way the light shines on your skin, the feel of the wind, the almost inaudible noise of what's happening in the distant.

It is a library beyond conscious memory, and the key is knowing how to access it. So, even while we have consciously forgotten about our creative, imaginative, and infinite selves, there is a part of us that still remembers. It has always been there and always will be—a place where our five-year-old selves still dances, dreams and believes in magic.

Settle in, relax your forehead, jaw, and shoulders. It's amazing how much tension we hold in our bodies, without realizing. Notice your scalp, relax that too.

As you sink into letting go of the tension in your body, notice as it also melts away the expectations of the world. The more you try to think about it, the further it gets. Move deeper into this feeling, letting go again and again. The more you let go, the more you allow yourself to remember.

Remember the way you once laughed—unrestrained, full of wonder, and without inhibition.

Remember the way the world stretched out before you like an endless horizon, full of promise. Untainted by doubt. Untouched by fear. Unknown to shame.

Remember when you didn't question your worth. When you had nothing to prove. That's right. There was magic in the air around you. Boundless dreams, untouched spirit. That little mini you, always there, still there, waiting for you to come home.

Now compare this feeling with the world's obsession with *thinking*. We are taught to *think*, we are rewarded to *think*, academia and work grades us by how well we *think*.

Very different right?

Because there's no award for *feeling*, coming home to yourself can feel foreign and unfamiliar. It is not a way of being that people are used to hence it may even cause concern for those around you. But, at some point, coming home to yourself becomes the single most important mission of your life, for without it, life is little more than a busy state of constantly *doing* while never knowing what you are doing it for.

When we think about permission, we usually float back to a time when we had to ask permission from authority. Permission to go to the bathroom in the middle of class, permission to have a friend over for a sleepover, permission to leave work early.

How often though do we give ourselves permission to be the author of our lives?

Permission to slow down, permission to take a stand for yourself, even if it upsets the people you love, knowing that those that really love you will get it eventually, just not right now. Or the permission to course correct in a way that sings to your heart, even if it comes with being misunderstood. The permission to be misunderstood!

To feel alive, we must dare to dream again, to wonder, to change pace, so we can return to the clarity we lost sight of while we were busy racing through each day.

We were conditioned to be busy, and if we weren't, we're lazy, so it's normal to feel guilty when we slow down. The irony, however, is that the path to remembering yourself may feel 'wrong' because it goes against everything we have been taught.

While the outward and inward paths have similarities, they move in opposite directions—one into the quiet space of our aliveness, the other towards the noise of the world—each requiring its own way of traveling, its own rhythm, its own pace. The way outward and inward must be travelled differently. The fervour and intensity we use to travel outwards is not useful when travelling inwards. The way outwards came with signposts and beaten tracks; the way inwards comes with a blindfold and must be sensed through feeling and intuition.

Begin to pay attention to the small things. Look into the faces of passerby, knowing that they have a story as rich and complicated as your own. Connect with their aliveness, knowing they have fears, hopes and heartaches, just like us. Knowing that they are also doing their best with what they have, just like us. Knowing that they want to be happy, just like us. There is a beautiful word that describes this: sonder.

Our shared aliveness is the essence of Life.

When you begin to reconnect with Life, it will feel subtle at first—like the first light of dawn creeping over the horizon. Depending on the depth of your conditioning, it may take some time to feel this shift, but you will. Moreover, if you take time to slow down and continually connect with that feeling, it will grow.

Unlike the linear upward trajectory we are used to, our journey home to ourselves is nurtured by awareness and openness. The more we try to control it, measure it, or compare it, the more it slips away from us. If the way we piled on conditioning was through expectations, then to remove it requires the opposite. We must let go of the way we expect the world to be to return to ourselves. It means to recognize the layers of dust that has piled on our once bright light bulb and to go through the process of cleaning them off, layer by layer.

The light in you was never contingent on what you achieved, because you shined bright to begin with. Even though we can't see the sun on a cloudy day, it still shines behind it, as bright as ever. You were born shining, full of love, and creative wonder. You were always whole—it never changed.

That was, and will remain, your greatest contribution to the world: the purity of your light—unfiltered and uncovered. The way beyond belonging is back to where it all began. The longer you stay on the wrong highway, the more tolls you pay to get home.

Your journey home begins now.

Beyonding

Welcome home. It's time to remember everything that is you. The you that belonged to yourself, before you belonged anywhere else.

In the doorway below, create a representation of what you're returning home to in any form you wish. What will you start saying yes to? What will you now say no to? What forgotten childlike wonders are you ready to welcome back? If your inner voice was a physical place, what's in that room?

References

1 Hanh, T. N. (2014). No mud, no lotus: The art of transforming suffering. Parallax Press.

2 Breakpoint and Beyond: Mastering the Future Today by George Land and Beth Jarman (https://www.youtube.com/watch?v=ZfKMq-rYtnc)

3 Milgram, S. (1963). Behavioural study of obedience. The Journal of abnormal and social psychology, 67(4), 371.

4 Brain Games Conformity Waiting Room (https://www.youtube.com/watch?v=X6kWygqR0L8&t=9s)

5 Maier, S. F., & Seligman, M. E. (1976). Learned helplessness: theory and evidence. Journal of experimental psychology: general, 105(1), 3.

6 Asch, S. E. (1956). Studies of independence and conformity: I. A minority of one against a unanimous majority. Psychological monographs: General and applied, 70(9), 1

7 Dunbar, R. I. (1992). Neocortex size as a constraint on group size in primates. Journal of human evolution, 22(6), 469-493.

8 Cohen, S., & Wills, T. A. (1985). Stress, social support, and the buffering hypothesis. Psychological bulletin, 98(2), 310.

9 Tolle, E. (2004). The power of now: A guide to spiritual enlightenment. New World Library.

10 Piaget, J. (2013). The construction of reality in the child. Routledge.

11 Lord, R. G., & Maher, K. J. (1991). Cognitive theory in industrial and organizational psychology. Handbook of Industrial and Organizational Psychology, 2, 1-62.

12 Reicher, S. D., Templeton, A., Neville, F., Ferrari, L., & Drury, J. (2016). Core disgust is attenuated by ingroup relations. Proceedings of the National Academy of Sciences, 113(10), 2631-2635.

13 Brown, D. (2021). A Book of Secrets. Penguin. Chapter 1 – Knowing Everything.

14 Livesay, V. T. (2013). Exploring the paradoxical role and experience of fallback in developmental theory

15 Festinger, L., Riecken, H. W., & Schachter, S. (2008). When prophecy fails. Pinter & Martin Publishers.

16 Dawson, L. L. (1999). When prophecy fails and faith persists: A theoretical overview. Nova Religio, 3(1), 60-82. https://doi.org/10.1525/nr.1999.3.1.60

17 Bregman, R. (2020). Humankind: A hopeful history. Bloomsbury Publishing.

18 Golden Buzzer: Nightbirde's Original Song Makes Simon Cowell Emotional – America's Got Talent 2021 (https://www.youtube.com/watch?v=CZJvBfoHDk0)

19 Ryan, R. M., & Deci, E. L. (2000). Self-determination theory and the facilitation of intrinsic motivation, social development, and well-being. American psychologist, 55(1), 68.

20 Lykken, D., & Tellegen, A. (1996). Happiness is a stochastic phenomenon. Psychological science, 7(3), 186-189.

21 Rotter, J. B. (1966). Generalized expectancies for internal versus External control of Reinforcement. Psychological Monographs, 80.

22 Rotter, J. B. (1954). Social Learning and Clinical Psychology. Johnson Reprint Corporation.

23 Roberts, A. R., Levine, E. E., & Sezer, O. (2021). Hiding success. Journal of Personality and Social Psychology, 120(5), 1261.

24 McKinsey & Company, & LeanIn.Org. (2022). Women in the workplace 2022. McKinsey & Company.

25 The Backwards Brain Bicycle – Smarter Every Day 133 (https://www.youtube.com/watch?v=MFzDaBzBlL0)

26 #IamRemarkable (https://www.rmrkblty.org/iamremarkable/our-story)

27 Mentoring SG (https://mentoring.sg/mentoring-culture)

28 Verian, Mentoring SG, National Youth Council and Ministry of Culture, Community & Youth (2025). State of Youth Mentoring in Singapore.

PENGUIN BOOKS

EMILIA FROM BEYOND

Shyra N is a storyteller at heart, whose writing is shaped by a deep curiosity about the complexities of human emotion and experience. Her creative works explore the quieter, messier moments of life: how they shape who we are and who we choose to become. She believes every woman has the potential to be the hero of her own story, a conviction that inspires her to craft strong, multidimensional female characters unafraid to defy expectations and embrace their individuality. Outside of writing, she enjoys watching dramas and anime, playing video games, and seeking out narratives that spark her imagination.